New DESIGNS for CHURCH LEADERSHIP

David S. Luecke

Publishing House
St. Louis

BV
652.1
.L84
1990

Unless otherwise noted, the Scripture quotations in this publication are from *The Holy Bible: NEW INTERNATIONAL VERSION*, © 1973, 1978, 1984 by the International Bible Society. Used by permission of Zondervan Bible Publishers.

Copyright © 1990 Concordia Publishing House
3558 S. Jefferson Avenue, St. Louis, MO 63118-3968
Manufactured in the United States of America

All rights reserved. No part of this publication may be reproduced, stored in a retrieval system, or transmitted, in any form or by any means, electronic, mechanical, photocopying, recording, or otherwise, without the prior written permission of Concordia Publishing House.

Library of Congress Cataloging in Publication Data

Luecke, David S., 1940–
    New designs for church leadership/David S. Luecke.
    p.   cm.
    Includes bibliographical references.
    ISBN 0-570-04546-0
    1. Christian leadership.   I. Title.
BV652.1.L84   1990   90-31681
253'.2—dc20   CIP

1 2 3 4 5 6 7 8 9 10   99 98 97 96 95 94 93 92 91 90

Contents

CONCORDIA COLLEGE LIBRARY
2811 N. E. HOLMAN ST.
PORTLAND, OREGON 97211

Acknowledgement __

Hundreds of people have contributed to this book even though they may not be aware of it. The imagery and approaches presented here emerged over the years from many interactive sessions devoted to helping church leaders gain insights from the world of management. In particular, the chapter materials came together as lectures in the doctor of ministry course on church management that I have taught to about 120 pastors at Fuller Theological Seminary.

Special acknowledgement must go to Dr. Norbert Oesch, pastor of St. John Lutheran Church, Orange, California, and chairperson of the Board for Parish Services of The Lutheran Church—Missouri Synod, and to Dr. Stephen J. Carter, formerly on the faculty at Concordia Theological Seminary, Fort Wayne, Indiana, and now vice-president of the editorial division at Concordia Publishing House. They invited me to participate in developing a study guide on church administration for a continuing education series sponsored by the Commission on Ministerial Growth and Support of the Missouri Synod. We spent two delightful retreats of several days each brainstorming the best approach to this topic. The book emerged as an addition and was considerably shaped by those discussions. It was originally meant as a companion piece to *Leadership for Pastors*, a program for clusters of pastors who study and share together. To assist pastors in teaching leadership to the congregations they serve, a lay study guide and an audio tape were also developed.

Even though the book originated out of a specific Lutheran program, the multidenominational nature of the Fuller Theological Seminary context assures that it is applicable to the leadership of a broad spectrum of Christian congregations. May it contribute to several degrees of better leadership and management of God's building process by pastors and the leaders of the churches they serve.

Chapter 1 ⎯⎯⎯⎯⎯⎯⎯

Images for Leaders of a Church

In his providence, God usually gives Christian congregations several leaders. The pastor is certainly one. Most others hold formal positions such as elder, deacon, or trustee. But some also lead informally as they involve others in getting things done.

A church with many leaders is blessed. Such people can make necessary and exciting things happen. But such a church also has the constant responsibility to engage these leaders fully and well. To do so, it has to understand the relationships between them. And all this leadership must continually strive to fulfill the mission for which Christ's church exists.

This book addresses those leadership challenges.

Church leadership is hard to discuss in general terms. In practice as well as in theory, a basic distinction among leaders is immediately made. There is the pastor (or pastoral staff), and there are the others. Thus, church leaders come in two forms:

church leaders = lay leaders + pastoral leader

The common name for leaders who are not pastors is lay leaders. The term *lay*, from the distinction between clergy and laity, can have connotations that work against a constructive understanding of the shared leadership task if *lay* means secondary or less important and suggests something other than real leadership. Real leadership is not the exclusive province of pastors, although they should be central to it. Church leadership is a shared endeavor among many people in their various positions and functions.

For pastors, church leadership is only one of several responsibilities. The term *leadership* is relatively new to the vocabulary of this field. It is increasingly used as traditional roles become more ambiguous and as the organizational dimensions of church life become more important. Pastors often understand church leadership as a call for better church administration, and

7

they are unsure how that relates to other aspects of their ministry, many of which seem to be more satisfying.

To improve church leadership, we must consider both pastoral leaders and lay leaders. But more attention will be given to pastors. They are the natural nucleus of a leadership team. In the understanding of the church's mission today, they have a clear role as the leader of leaders. And they often have the most distance to cover in fitting themselves into new leadership expectations.

Starting Where You Are

If you are a pastoral leader, check the statements that describe you:

1. Sometimes I feel overwhelmed by all the expectations of my ministry. Why aren't preaching and teaching enough?

2. I feel that I am losing my authority, and I am not sure how to get it back.

3. We have experienced some real successes at my church, and I want to know how to keep the momentum going.

4. I know that some of my members are disappointed because I am not a stronger leader for our church.

5. So many members need my care and counseling, and I want to know how to reduce the other demands on my time.

6. Many days I feel like a church technician just going through the motions.

7. My church has some members with real leadership potential; how can I channel that energy more effectively?

8. I was trained for more important work than administration, and I wish I did not have to do it.

9. I have many ideas for my church's ministry, but I am frustrated because so few get off the ground.

10. I am sure of God's calling to ministry, and I am looking for ways to be more faithful in doing it.

Most pastors will probably find that several of these statements reflect their situation as church leader. If you see yourself somewhere in those descriptions, you should find valuable help in the discussions that follow. They are aimed at offering concepts, insights, reference points, and practical applications that can make more sense out of the often confusing work of providing ministerial leadership for the life of a Christian congregation.

Some pastors always seem to "have it all together" in their

pastoral leadership. Rejoice and thank God if you are one. The following discussions can provide better handles for talking about what you do. You have much to offer your colleagues in ministry. Experience in continuing education for ministers does suggest that pastors typically approach issues of their leadership contribution with more negative feelings and doubts about themselves than with joy and confidence. What follows is intended to offer sources of potential affirmation and increased understanding. Out of new insights may also come some sparks of new excitement.

If you are a lay church leader, check the statements that fit you:

1. I want to be a better leader in my church, and I am looking for ways to improve.

2. I feel worn out because the same small group of leaders has to do everything.

3. I have more to offer my church than I am called on to give.

4. My church does not seem to have an overall sense of purpose beyond surviving from year to year.

5. I have considerable management experience to offer, but I can't seem to get our pastor interested.

6. We have lost momentum at our church, and we can't get it going again.

7. I am excited about our church's potential; we just have to learn to pull together.

8. I want to help our pastor be a stronger leader.

9. Our pastor is doing a great job; I want to give more encouragement.

10. We have to learn how to get more done in the time available.

Most church members who are active in leadership will find several statements that fit their situation. The concepts and insights that follow should help them, too. Church leadership can improve only when pastoral leaders and lay leaders grow together in their understanding of what they are doing. A shared vocabulary is basic. Readers whose pastor is using the distinctions and terms of the approach presented here can better know and contribute to the discussion. Readers whose pastor is not yet familiar with the terms will have a framework for getting a better hearing for their concerns.

Shifts in Leader Image

Pastors follow a special calling that God has been giving for thousands of years. They and other church leaders stand in a long and mighty progression of people whom God has used for good among those whom He continually gathers as His church. What should church leadership look like today?

The leadership images that pastors themselves have had of their work have shifted over the centuries and through many changes in culture. From century to century, the way pastors saw their work strongly influenced how the rest of church leadership was regarded. These shifts happened in response to changing needs of churches, as well as by assimilating differing leadership understandings that prevailed in the societies where churches found themselves.

Late 20th-century North America has seen striking shifts in leadership images in political, business, and other spheres. Christian churches have encountered new and trying circumstances for ministry in social contexts of often dramatic change. Most long-established denominations witnessed decline in membership and vitality and a corresponding loss of leadership confidence. Many newer churches and denominations are seeing growth but miss the tested leadership experience that gives stability to their gains.

It is little wonder that providing effective church leadership is a source of confusion and frustration in many churches today. Leaders, especially pastors, have to cope with images that do not seem to fit together. The term *leadership* itself is relatively new on the scene of preparation for church ministry. Few seminary catalogs of earlier years mentioned it. The term is now a popular abstract concept for a complicated set of relationships, and that abstraction has little direct parallel in Scripture or in the church and general literature of former eras.

An image of leadership is really made up of three component images. Each of these in turn has many possibilities. The three components are:

Images for the leaders
Images for the followers
Images for what they are trying to do

The following chapters will identify and discuss several pos-

10

sible guiding images for these components, beginning especially with images of the pastor as leader.

These discussions will be more than just a survey. They are offered with the conviction that several of the possibilities are particularly appropriate and fruitful for church leadership in the current circumstances of Protestant churches in North America.

Themes

Building, fellowship, and mission are the major themes. The most basic theme to unify the featured images is *building*, as in building a house or building the body of believers as a fellowship. This is an important Scriptural theme. It was a favorite of the apostle Paul, who used variations of it repeatedly in verbalizing his leadership intentions for the many congregations to which he ministered. Truly surprising is how little this theme was picked up and used by the generations of church leaders who followed. The heritage for church leadership conveys minimal conscious development of the extensive implications of this self-identity for pastoral leaders.

The idea of building raises the question of what is to be built. Theologically, it is to be the body of Christ, as Paul says in Eph. 4:12. The more concrete object of attention will be *fellowship*. This thrust is present in the Greek word that Paul used for "building," which literally means to build a house or a household. Fellowship can be understood in a specific or a general sense. Acts of friendly sharing are one form of fellowship; that is what takes place in a church "fellowship hall." But the concept has a much broader and more basic meaning, describing the whole community of believers gathered in a local church. In Paul's time these often were extended households. Today we recognize especially a small local congregation as a "fellowship," or basic unit of a church. Larger congregations may have several fellowship units.

The popularity of the term today is a disadvantage for present purposes because fellowship is often trivialized to mean only social interaction. For our purposes it is better understood as a description of a congregation rather than just people having good times together. Fellowship is not a separate function of church life. It is all of church life. It is the local body of Christ in action.

The third fundamental theme is *mission*, as in "the church exists for mission." Relevant images are less concrete, but the challenge is nonetheless real. Churches and their leaders can func-

11

tion with little consciousness of mission beyond maintaining themselves faithfully. But God calls his people to a larger perspective of outreach and service. In the changing circumstances of church life today, the mission or missions for a church cannot be taken for granted. Actually, in the current usage of the word, there is little reason to talk about leadership where there is little sense of compelling mission.

There is increasing conviction among American Protestants that the compelling mission of the church today has something to do with growth in outreach. Church growth as a study and practice has gained increasing acceptance, although valid concerns have been raised about some manifestations and principles of the movement. Building a fellowship for mission, as presented here, has many parallels with Church growth emphases. Leadership for one can share much in common with leadership for the other.

The theme and images of fellowship building provide a comprehensive focus for the life and work of a church. Furthermore, church *building* is a human activity for which God has explicitly called church leaders. Church *growth* is not something human leaders can do. God provides the growth wherever it happens, and it is important for church leaders to avoid the temptation to think that they can "grow" a church. But they can strive to build on the foundation God offers, and they need to be careful how they build (1 Cor. 3:10). Sharpening their self-image as builder/pastor is an especially appropriate step in improving the leadership that pastors strive to provide.

Ministry and Management

Much of what follows will come from the literature of management, or, more particularly, of management education. Helping people become better managers and leaders is the fundamental task of one of the largest educational specialties in higher education—schools of business administration. There are many parallels between the leadership offered by managers and by ministers. But church leadership is not just a subsection of management like hospital or school administration. There is much more to churches than just their organization, and there is much more especially to pastoral leadership than church administration.

The approach here will be to present first the challenges of leading a church as they appear in churches, in Scripture, and in a church leader's life. To this will be brought insights from the experience of leaders in other contexts, intended mostly to clarify what to look for and how to react to what is happening in the interactions of those who are to be led.

The relation between ministry and management is tenuous in the perspective of many pastors. On the one hand, there is usually a common-sense willingness to learn practical steps toward better results. On the other hand, there is often a strong concern that the special nature and emphases of church ministry not be lost. Most presentations of management for ministers deserve skepticism. They start with what managers do and have learned and then encourage ministers to do likewise. It is usually readily acknowledged that leaders will have to adapt the program to fit their church, but they are usually on their own to do so. And they are justifiably concerned that they may be seduced into unfaithfulness if they are not careful. Or the management posture might be that when the leaders present the goals for the church, management expertise can help figure out how to accomplish them. But pastoral leaders often are not confident that they know the goals, or more precisely, that they know how to translate them from theological language into management language.

In a word, what is lacking is integration. Integration of ministry and management is a fundamental purpose for the discussions that follow. The approach comes from the writer's 20 years of experience trying to teach and help ministers gain more management skills for church leadership. Experience says that it is best to start with ministry, its Scriptural base, and its context. Then add doses of management insights as appropriate.

Analysis, How-to Manuals, and Inspiration

Experience also indicates that the best way to help someone become a better leader is to offer tools for analysis. This is not just the writer's personal experience but the basic commitment of management education. The better the business school, the higher the expectations for analytical rigor. This is because the circumstances encountered and the outcomes sought vary so much from organization to organization and over time. The search for the one best way of managing something is long over. There is no one way that will always work. Leader effectiveness today depends on the ability to see and assess what is happening and to select the best response from a variety of options. Seeing and assessing are fundamental, as is knowing how to look for the options.

The emphasis on images in these chapters reflects a high commitment to offering analytical tools to church leaders so they can see, assess, and discover how to respond as leaders. The analytical framework does not demand rigor to get at it, but it certainly invites rigor for those inclined toward further pursuit. The framework simply offers handles to categories and reference points for discussion of common experiences in church leadership. Academics talk about "paradigms" to describe the perceptual categories in common use. The present work is intended to "shift paradigms" for church leadership. Shifting images means almost the same thing.

The material will have served its purpose if the reader occasionally says, "Yes, now I see; that explains what I have been trying to get at." The outcome will be even better if the reader acquires a few more key words that facilitate productive discussion with other church leaders. Most of the featured vocabulary is "user friendly."

One common alternative for writing about church leadership and administration is to present a how-to manual that explains in great detail the steps to be taken in leading one or another phase of church life, such as how to run a stewardship campaign or how to organize an office. This is not a how-to manual, although the discussion will continually try to point out the general direction for *how to* get better at meeting one challenge or another. Such manuals are available and several are useful, but they tend to be oriented toward a specific denominational approach.

Another common approach could be called *inspirational*. It would feature descriptions of what church leaders ought to try to do. Exhortation from Scripture is common. This is usually accompanied by sharing the experiences and observations of ministers who are recognized as successful at leading churches. The present book offers few stories; it expects the readers to fill in their own. The difficulty with the "this-is-how-I-do-it" genre of leadership literature is that little recognition is typically given to the special circumstances and unique personality of the one whose leadership is featured. Trying to copy someone else's style and approach can be frustrating to church leaders who have different personalities and face different circumstances.

14

But inspiration is important. The present offering will look to Scripture for most of that. It also trusts that the reader will gain greater self-confidence from the framework and insights that help make sense out of that often confusing world of church leadership. The final chapter directly addresses enthusiasm for church leadership.

Most chapters will have exploration topics supplementing the presentation of the basic images. These featured images are meant to guide thinking about how better to see the tasks and challenges of leading a church and of being faithful to one's calling as a minister of God. The explorations will sometimes discuss where that image originates or what some alternatives are.

Exploration Topic A: New Testament Images for Leader Positions

Of course, any faithful discussion of church leader images has to start with God's Word. Especially important are the images He led the early Christian church to use.

Two types are most helpful: images that identify leader positions and images that are analogous to other leaders in society. Although position titles most readily come to mind in a discussion of leadership, it is the analogies that will best open up fresh insights for church leadership today.

The images featured in this exploration topic are: elder, bishop, deacon, and apostle, Exploration Topic B considers the leader analogies of shepherd, steward, helmsman, and builder.

A search for an organizational chart of the New Testament church will end in frustration. Such position consciousness is more characteristic of Christian churches in later centuries, leaving churches of today a legacy of many different structures after which to pattern themselves. The structure of the first-century church developed over time, and so did the status and relationships of its leaders. Thus the various New Testament writers use position images whose meanings often were not fixed or precise at the time of writing.

Elder

The basic leader status designation was *elder* (in Greek, *presbuteros*, or older person). The term was carried over from the

15

Jewish culture but was also used in Greek practice. It described those who by virtue of their wisdom and forcefulness, gained with or without many years of experience, were recognized as leaders that a community could follow. It comes closest to being a generic description comparable to "leader" today. A congregation could have more than one elder (Acts 20:17), and most undoubtedly did. The leadership of elders was recognized by an act that established order (Acts 14:23 and Titus 1:5, where older versions translate the verb as "to ordain"). How formal such a ceremony was is not clear. Undoubtedly many of the individuals named in the epistles as leaders and coworkers were elders.

Among the New Testament status categories, elder probably comes closest to describing the status of most ordained pastors today. They hold a special office among other recognized leaders of a congregation.

Bishop

Of higher status was *bishop,* a term whose function is conveyed by the word "overseer," the literal meaning of the Greek *episcopos. Supervisor* from the Latin means the same thing. The term was much used in Greek literature. It appears in Phil. 1:1; 1 Tim. 3:1; and Titus 1:7. A common view of church historians is that the overseer was originally one of the elders and was charged with oversight of the common meals and the offerings of the faithful. Over time a bishop "oversaw" several congregations, and a higher status came to be recognized.

For historical reasons, many Protestants today avoid the term *bishop.* But there is ample New Testament precedent for using it at the local level. The pastor of today may be seen as holding a different office from other elders by virtue of picking up the function of overseeing the life of a church. Not to be overlooked is the early emphasis on administrative supervision.

Deacon

A *deacon* usually held lower status than an elder. A different status is apparent in Acts 6, where Stephen and six others were designated to serve by administering the food shared in common by the Jerusalem church. "Deacon" in Greek means *servant.* The Latin form is *minister,* or "lesser one" (from *minor*). Deacons dealt with the most practical aspects of leadership. As status became more regularized after the New Testament era, deacons were a third order of recognized leader after bishop and elder. By using the word *minister*, pastors today identify with the deacon, but the lower status and practical dimension of the early ministry of the deacon are often not emphasized.

Apostle

Apostle was clearly the highest status in the early church. It was used for the "sent ones" whose leadership was commissioned directly by Christ. In the general sense of an ambassador to others (the Latin-derived form for *apostle*) with broad powers, the image is available today. But strong church tradition reserves the term *apostle* for the limited number of first-generation leaders.

Over subsequent centuries several changes took place in the tripartite ranking of bishop, elder, and deacon. The image of *priest*, with its emphasis on the ritual life of the community, gained dominance and supplanted the general leader category of elder. Significantly, the English word *priest* is derived from *presbuteros*, the Greek word that is translated as "elder." By the Middle Ages, the classical church leader pattern of bishop, priest, and deacon was firmly in place.

The position of the priest came to be seen as strictly separated from that of other Christians, and church leadership eventually passed out of reach of ordinary Christians who lost access to the elite, carefully controlled status of the priestly clergy in the rank of bishop, priest, and deacon. Everyone else became the laity, the common people, from whom leadership in church matters was no longer expected.

A fundamental contribution of the Protestant Reformation is belief in the priesthood of all believers. The status of a priestly clergy standing between God and the laity was removed. Instead, the clergy were seen as holding an office established by God to carry out publicly the functions of ministry given to the whole church. Out of this theological understanding has come the insight, in need of renewal from time to time, that various aspects of church leadership are to be shared among all the people to whom God has given the ability to lead. Some leaders, ordained as pastors, are called to carry out special spiritual responsibilities. Others make specific contributions as they are able and are recognized. All members of the body can serve as true leaders.

Several other leadership terms are used by the apostle Paul

17

in Rom. 12, 1 Cor. 12, and Eph. 4. They include apostles, prophets, evangelists, pastors and teachers, presiders, and administrators (plus servers, encouragers, contributors, healers, helpers, workers of miracles, speakers in tongues, interpreters). Three significant features of these lists can be noted. First, the positions of bishop, elder, and deacon are not mentioned, although apostle is. Second, the listings are not consistent in the three references. Third, each listing offers examples of the differing gifts of grace God gives his church through the Holy Spirit.

These factors have led some New Testament scholars to conclude that Paul is describing not so much leadership positions as functions—not who the different leaders are but what they do. For example, Gunther Bornkamm notes:

> *Paul for the most part refers to leaders of the churches in terms of function rather than office. He enjoins obedience to them but more because of their ministry than their status. The constitutional principle is that of a plurality of gifts. This does not rule out, however, the existence of bishops and deacons.*[1]

Perhaps as a reflection of this understanding of leadership in general, Paul in his other writing makes little reference to the general position of elder, although he writes about bishops and deacons. Presumably many of the functional leaders were elders. One common interpretation is that the positions of bishop and deacon describe leaders who stayed in one fellowship, while those who made special and particularly Word-related contributions, such as prophets or evangelists, moved among different groups. Presumably, local elders/leaders also exercised one or another of these functional gifts. They probably showed a dominance of teaching, pastoring, and administering contributions.

Church leaders of today who are seeking greater congruence in their self-image as leader can find Paul's approach affirming and liberating. The pastoral ministry has less of the image of a job description to fit into and is more the availability of an opportunity to stress the leadership that comes to an individual because of the gift of the Holy Spirit and the call of the church. The challenge is for each leader to contribute what God has uniquely given to each person to share. That is possible when one

---

[1] Gunther Bornkamm, *Theological Dictionary of the New Testament*, ed. Gerhard Kittel, Gerhard Friedrich, and Geoffrey Bromily (Grand Rapids, Mich.: Eerdmans, 1985), s.v. *"presbus."*

recognizes that in God's providence a gathering of Christians will have many leaders with complementary contributions to make, not just one who has to do it all. In most churches today pastoral leaders cannot ignore the general responsibility that goes with local leadership, but they can also be confident in choosing images of leadership functions that they will personally stress.

The heritage of pastoral leadership images available today has not featured this liberating view of church leadership as involving diverse contributions from many people. Leadership practices in the societies of previous centuries were very conscious of status, and functional diversity was easily overlooked. Also, classical Protestantism did not operate with a well-developed theology of gifts of the Spirit. Rediscovery of Paul's emphasis has largely been a phenomenon of the church only in the latter half of the 20th century.

How providential is that rediscovery! It comes just at a time when an older consensus of expectations for a church's leadership is faltering. A new emphasis on functional gifts of the Spirit can facilitate a shift in self-image for both pastoral and lay leaders.

Exploration Topic B: Images from Leader Analogies

In teaching about leadership, New Testament writers used several helpful terms that go beyond position or function. These have a literal base that called forth leadership images easily recognizable in the society the readers knew. These analogies can open up productive insights for church leaders committed to Biblical foundations for their ministry. The purposeful use of analogy is most clearly seen in 1 Cor. 3:10: "By the grace God has given me, I laid a foundation as an expert builder, and someone else is building on it." This is the key passage for the *builder* analogy to be featured. The apostle Paul uses the image and terminology of "builder" and "building" 32 times. The implications for today are the subject of the subsequent chapters.

Most well-known is the analogy of *shepherd* or, in Latin, *pastor*. The preservation thrust of this image presents a possible contrast to that of builder. Although used extensively to describe the relationship between God and His people, the image is applied explicitly to church leaders only three times.

Whatever kind of leadership a church needs today, administration will be a part of it. Pastoral ministers typically report spending up to 40 percent of their time in this activity. Many people in our highly organized modern society can think only with difficulty of any other leadership besides that of administrators. There is more, of course, as will be developed. But seldom is there effective church leadership without it.

Two New Testament leader analogies offer especially helpful self-identity for doing this work. One is the *steward*, or *manager*. Jesus makes the direct reference in Luke 12:42 (also Matt. 24:45), where he identifies "the faithful and wise manager" (NIV), whom the master puts in charge of his servants to give them their food at the right time. See also Luke 16:1–12. In his usual way, Paul expands the image to describe leadership in the church.

The other administrative leader analogy is the *helmsman*, one of God's special gifts to a church, as listed in 1 Cor. 12:28 ("those with gifts of administration" in the NIV).

Steward (Manager)

The Greek word for "steward" is *oikonomos*. The first part, *oikos*, means "house" or "household." We will hear much more about *oikos* in the next chapter, which emphasizes the expanded sense of household as the basic fellowship group of the church. The last part, *nomos*, means something assigned or apportioned out. Thus the steward is the leader—the administrator—who looks after the distribution of things within a household. That process is the essence of what is described in the English word "economy" (from *oikonomia*)—the distribution of goods and services in a society. In recognition of that reference point in economics, "steward" can quite properly be translated as "manager," the modern term applied originally to those who operate economic activity. Paul would have had this conventional sense in mind as he conveyed to the Romans the greetings of Erastus, the city manager (Rom. 16:23).

This image of church leaders appears in three places. It is used explicitly as an analogy in Titus: "Since an overseer is entrusted with God's work, he must be blameless" (Tit. 1:7). Remember that in the earliest church the bishop was probably the head elder or leader for a local church, in a capacity not much different from that of the senior pastor of a typical congregation today. Then hear this charge as encouragement for a pastoral minister to be like a steward, administrator, or manager.

20

Paul tells the Corinthians that he wants their leaders to be considered by people "as servants of Christ and as those entrusted (*oikonomoi*) with the secret things of God." In this respect he says that "those who have been given a trust must prove faithful" (1 Cor. 4:1–2). In the Latin Bible, the "secret things of God" were called *sacramenta*. Hence comes the classical description for the work of pastors as, in addition to preaching the Gospel, administering the sacraments. In the earlier discussion of bishop, it was noted that by the time of Ignatius in the early second century, the bishop was charged with "overseeing" or supervising the common meals, especially the sacrament of the Lord's Supper. Thus he functioned according to the image of an administrator or steward for the church.

Basic to the image is the presence of resources that need to be apportioned to others. In the church the sacraments are fundamental resources from God. Other resources are the many different contributions that members make in the body of Christ. These are manifestations of the Spirit, the spiritual gifts (*charismata*) to the church from members acting in diverse ways for the common good as they are led by the Spirit (1 Cor. 3:7–14). Paul most clearly recognized and described this resource.

The apostle Peter knew the administrative implications, and he gives us the third use of the steward image. Such contributions need to be distributed or apportioned. After encouraging his readers to exercise their diverse gifts, he urges them to minister to each other "as good stewards of the grace of God" (1 Pet. 4:10 RSV). Actually, the word for "grace" means the gifts of grace (*charismata*). Although the stewardship responsibility starts with each person, it extends to all in this common effort. Thus we can see Peter calling for good managers who can guide the contributions of individuals to where they can best serve the common good.

It is the presence of such diverse activity in need of coordination that makes effective administrative leadership so necessary also for churches today.

Helmsman

This image appears twice in the New Testament. Once it occurs with the literal meaning of the pilot of a ship, in this case the Alexandrian ship sailing for Italy with the prisoner Paul

21

aboard. The helmsman is distinguished from the ship owner (Acts 27:11).

This is the image Paul highlights in his listing of functional parts of the body of Christ in 1 Cor. 12:27–28. After the Word-gifted apostles, prophets, and teachers come the miracle workers and those with the gifts of healing, doing helpful deeds, *helmsmanship* ("those with gifts of administration"), and diversities of tongues. When he goes on to ask rhetorically whether all members do each of these activities, he significantly refrains from asking whether all do the navigating of the body. It is apparently obvious that only a few can do that.

Navigating is the key part of this analogy for leadership. The helmsman was not the owner of the ship and did not set the destination. But he was more than simply the sailor at the rudder. In ancient sailing he was more like the highly experienced captain of the ship, the pilot, who was responsible for getting the ship and all aboard to their destination, which was determined by the owner. This broad sense of responsibility for others and for the achievement of purpose led older Bible versions to translate helmsmanship as "government." Happily, modern translations (RSV, NIV) call it "administration."

Navigation can be seen as having three components. These three can also be seen in the modern application of the Greek word for helmsmanship, *kubernēsis*, to the engineering science of automated controls, called cybernetics. A thermostat is a simple cybernetic or navigation device. The steps are:

1. *Identifying the destination.* Although someone else may envision where the ship is to go, the helmsman has to know precisely where the destination is in relation to the surrounding geography. This step of pinpointing is similar to specifying for a room thermostat that the desired temperature should be a comfortable 72 degrees.

2. *Measuring progress.* The navigator continually measures the current position of the ship on its journey, determining where it is in relation to where it started and where it is going. A thermostat does this with a thermometer that constantly measures current temperature in the room.

3. *Adjusting course.* If the ship strays off course or is supposed to turn, the helmsman shifts the rudder or changes the speed to get it back on course. When the thermometer registers

temperature different from 72 degrees, the thermostat switches on a furnace or an air conditioner.

The same three steps are at the heart of the modern practice of management. The desired outcome for a managed activity or department is stated as clearly as possible, preferably in quantified terms such as an annual number of widgets produced or a percentage increase in revenue. Progress toward that objective is measured in weekly or monthly reports of actual results. When a departure from the plan becomes evident, the manager is expected to make changes in what is going on, perhaps by increasing effort or deferring activity that is less central to achieving the objective.

How appropriate is this analogy for providing leadership for a congregation? It will have little relevance if a church is not striving for a known destination beyond where it is at the time. In that case, the builder analogy also has little relevance. When a church has a vision and plans for achieving it, then leaders have to be responsible for keeping the various efforts of that congregation aimed along the chosen course. Helmsmanship will involve many leaders of a church in assessing progress and trying to make adjustments here and there. Necessarily, a pastoral leader intent on a building ministry will want to stay close to this ongoing work of outcome-oriented administration.

Shepherd

As used extensively in the Old Testament, the image of shepherd relates to activities that include feeding, watering, leading, watching over, caring for, seeking out, rescuing, and gathering his flock, bringing back the strong, binding up the crippled, strengthening the weak, and carrying the lambs in his bosom.[2] In the image of the Good Shepherd, Jesus cares for His sheep and is selfless in laying down His life for them. He knows them well and protects them (John 10:1–18).

As noted earlier, this image is explicitly applied to Christian church leaders three times. Elders are exhorted to be shepherds in Acts 20:28 and 1 Peter 5:2. The image is listed in Eph. 4:11 but drops out of the comparable list in 1 Cor. 12:28. In these uses

---

[2] P. L. Garber, *International Standard Bible Encyclopedia*, ed. Geoffrey Bromily (Grand Rapids, Mich.: Eerdmans, 1988), s.v. "sheep."

it does not receive amplification. Interpretation generally relates to Jesus' application of the term to Himself.

Clearly, the shepherd image is well loved and used among Christian leaders today, especially those who are called to the pastoral office. The word "pastor" comes from the Latin for shepherd, and the current use of "Pastor" as a preferred title (as in Pastor John Smith) indicates the appeal of this image. It can be noted, however, that although the shepherd image has always been present in the history of the Christian ministry, the use of the term as a position designation or a formal title is fairly recent. Its elevation to the preferred image and title occurred among 18th-century German Lutheran pietists, who were seeking to narrow the traditional gap between ordained minister and ordinary Christian. They shifted the leadership image to bring about a renewed vision of closer, more supportive relationships.[3]

In relation to the builder theme, one can observe that the shepherd image places more emphasis on maintaining than on building. The shepherd takes care of the sheep who are assigned to his care. He does not go out looking for new and different sheep. Featured shepherding activities are preservation oriented: watching over, caring for, rescuing, gathering, binding up the crippled, and strengthening the weak.

Especially as used today, building is different from maintaining. To maintain is to keep something as good as it was before, preserving it by regularly cleaning, repairing, and restoring what gets frayed, worn down, or reduced over time (rescuing, binding up, etc.). Building involves putting together something that was not there before by starting where there was nothing or by adding new parts to what already exists.

In current discussions of ministry, a distinction is sometimes made between doing maintenance ministry and doing building ministry. Often the reference to the maintenance focus is disparaging, as if it were insufficiently challenging or worthwhile, but that is not a Scriptural view. To focus on building does not mean to diminish the importance of preserving what already exists, but it does mean that preserving is not the sole end in itself.

The Lord looks on preservation as necessary and worthwhile. This amounts to guarding and protecting the faith and the spir-

---

[3] James H. Pragman, *Traditions of Ministry* (St. Louis: Concordia Publishing House, 1983), 126.

itual life of those for whom God holds the leaders accountable (Heb. 13:17). Timothy was charged to "guard what has been entrusted to your care" (1 Tim. 6:20) and to "keep [what you have heard from me] as the pattern of sound teaching" (2 Tim 1:13). Of the Pauline leadership functions, showing mercy (Rom. 12:8) and healing (1 Cor. 12:9) are closely related to maintenance work within the body of Christ. Teaching historically has had much of that thrust, especially when concentrated on instruction in the rudiments of the faith that is being passed on in the body of Christ. As Paul told Timothy, orthodoxy (right teaching) among those gathered is something to be preserved and maintained.

In the leadership functions listed in Eph. 4, "pastor" is closely associated with "teacher." The sense of maintenance is probably most captured today in the concept of pastoral care, including pastoral counseling. Just as many congregations have members gifted to teach in the church, churches are finding many members gifted to provide care and counseling.

The image of pastor, with or without its shepherd reference, is deeply embedded in the self-concept of many today. With it goes a tendency to think of leadership as being supportive of the church members at hand, caring for them individually and maintaining their patterns of relationships. In no way can other leadership images be allowed to detract from this ministry.

Yet the pastor image can be challenged as incomplete. That stance flows directly from the mission task so clearly enunciated by Paul in the theme of building the body. The pastor image could be stretched and adapted to include this thrust to more mission outreach and upbuilding. Perhaps over time it will move that way in general understanding. But the dual thrust of building and maintaining can probably best be kept in focus by featuring the two images: Pastor, yes—builder, too. One might even wonder whether Paul would say: Builder, yes—pastor, too.

Having clarified leadership positions and analogies in the New Testament context, we are now ready to concentrate on the image of builder.

Chapter 2 _____

Church Leaders as Fellowship Builders

Consider these builders:

Frank Casper is a journeyman carpenter. He describes his work this way:

> *I love the feel and smell of wood. It says something can be built and I like to do that. It is a real thrill to walk onto a job site and see the different stacks of lumber ready to be cut and fit together. They tell me there's important work to do. Some people might think two-by-fours or two-by-eights are all the same, but they aren't. They can be warped or split and have knots in the wrong places. I like having the skill to deal with that and all the other challenges of getting everything together without wasting time.*
>
> *Building houses is my favorite work. Every day is a little different. Figuring out what has to be done for floors, walls, roof and trim keeps me on my toes. Sometimes I can get a change of pace with simple electrical or plumbing work. Best of all is seeing the progress. The days can be long and tiring, but I usually go home satisfied that I made something important with my own hands.*

Roger Hensley is a licensed contractor. He comments:

> *I used to be a carpenter, but I wanted to take on more responsibility. I might have a hammer in my hand now and then, but not often. I spend much of my time being sure others get the work done. This means I deal a lot with tradesmen and subcontractors in the various specialties. You have to be careful who you get on a job or you can really get into trouble. I believe in finding the good ones, treating them fair, and then explaining what the project is and trusting them to do it right. Some are my good friends. There are definitely easier ways to make a living. But building is in my blood. I like the challenge. You have to be confident you can figure out all the problems that come up. You have to stay ahead to get the sequence right and*

keep the project on schedule. *It's surprising how many things can get in the way of bringing materials and workers together at the right time. You really have to keep a close eye on costs. Too much time or material in one area puts real pressure on another, and everything has to get done.*

Sometimes I take on commercial projects. I like house building best though, because it seems more worthwhile. Give me either a good custom job or a large-scale subdivision or apartment complex. I like thinking about all the families benefiting from what I do.

Sylvia Pitman, F.A.I.A., is an architect who says this about her work:

I'm a designer. My mind keeps thinking about how to give shape to space so that it fills a purpose and looks as welcoming as possible. My buildings need to be sturdy, of course, but I want them to be exciting, too. I'm always looking for ideas in other buildings I see. My work stays interesting because each project is different. Even though it may start out as just another apartment complex, every lot is different; square footage differs, and the result has to fit in with the surroundings. The owners have their own ideas, too. Custom houses are the most fun because I get to learn about the family and what makes them unique. Expansions are especially challenging because the new has to fit in with the old. The most anxiety and the greatest thrill happen around that time of the inspiration that fits everything together into the overall design. I like best doing the sketches and floor plans. Of course, the detailed construction plans have to be done, too. I'm thankful to get help with that. Builders are the backbone of a civilization. I'm glad to be one of them.

Paul of Tarsus, F.B. (Fellowship Builder)

The initials F.A.I.A. behind a name like Sylvia Pitman's are the definitive identification of a professional architect today. They stand for Fellow of the American Institute of Architects.

We could well put behind the apostle Paul's name the initials F.B. They would stand for Fellowship Builder. He was the most prominent founder of what we could call the Society for Fellowship Builders—the 1,950-year-old succession of Christian church leaders, both pastoral and lay, who concentrated on extending the church through the Gospel beyond whatever circumstances

27

they inherited at their time. Most would be members in retrospect, however, because the analogy of builder was seldom part of their formal self-identity.

By going back to the mission and ministry of Paul, we can uncover and regain a focus that offers coherence and productive insights for church leadership today. Paul called himself an "expert builder" (1 Cor. 3:10). Actually, the Greek word he used means architect. He deliberately chose the builder analogy to explain how he was leading. He even imputed the qualifier of a special kind of builder. Not just a *tektōn*, or carpenter, he saw himself as an *architektōn*, a primary or originating builder. We could say a designer.

His distinction invites a comparison with builders of today. Between the readily recognized carpenter and architect has emerged the contractor to deal with the complexities of modern building. The work of the contractor would be similar to that conveyed in the Biblical image of "steward." New perspectives on church leadership can come from considering carpenter ministry, contractor ministry, and architectural ministry.

The basic analogy is the building function. "Fellowship building" is a good translation of the Greek word *oikodomeō* that Paul used. In its verb and noun forms it appears in Paul's writings 32 times, occasionally with prefixes. Literally, it consists of words meaning "house" (*oikos*) and "to build" (*domeō*). It is usually translated simply "to build" or "building," but many times it is given the more general notion of "to edify" (from the literal Latin equivalent, available in English today as "edifice") in the sense of "to build up."

In Paul's time the word was commonly used in the literal sense when the object was a physical building. But it was also used in an extended sense in which the object of the activity was those who lived in a house, that is, a household or family. It is apparent that Paul saw himself involved in the ministry of building households. These were not just any household or family but those made up of believers sharing life in Christ.

His explicit reference can be found where he addresses a church at a particular individual's house: the church at Aquila and Priscilla's house in Ephesus (1 Cor. 16:19) and then in Rome (Rom. 16:3), at Philemon's house in Colossae (Philemon 2), and at Nympha's house in Laodicea (Col. 4:15). Warren Meeks notes that these household-based groups were the basic cells of the

Christian movement. He suggests that the group could extend far beyond immediate relatives.[1] A similar phenomenon can be seen today in the "house church movement" by which the Christian church has so rapidly expanded in mainland China. Today in America the extended household of a Christian leader is seldom the basic cell group of church life. Usually a small congregation serves that purpose, although there is increasing awareness that several different fellowship groups can function in the same local congregation. "Fellowship group" probably best gets at the meaning of Paul's *oikos* in *oikodomeō*. Thus, when Paul talks about building a house, we can properly understand him to be talking about building a fellowship of believers in Christ. Note that "fellowship" here means more than friendly interaction. It is the basic unit of church life, usually seen now as a congregation. The phrase "fellowship building" will be used in the following quotations that show Paul describing his ministry as that of a builder.

Paul as Architect

The key passage for this whole analogy is 1 Cor. 3:10. Here Paul explicitly identifies himself as architect, which is the Greek word he uses. It is usually translated as master or expert builder.

> *By the grace God has given me, I laid a foundation as an* architect, *and someone else is* building fellowship *on it. But each one should be careful how he* builds fellowship. *For no one can lay any foundation other than the one already laid, which is Jesus Christ. If any man* builds fellowship *on this foundation using gold, silver, costly stones, wood, hay or straw, his work will be shown for what it is. . . . If* the fellowship he has built *survives, he will receive his reward.* (1 Cor. 3:10–14; the terms in roman typeface are the author's translation of "expert builder" as "architect" and "build" as "build fellowship.")

Here Paul's architectural concern for the right beginnings, the best materials, and sturdy design are apparent. That he thinks like a designer who wants to keep options open can be seen even more clearly in Rom. 15:20, where he states his preference to preach the Gospel where Christ was not known, so that

---

[1] Warren Meeks, *The First Urban Christians* (Yale University Press, 1983), 75–77.

29

he would not have to build fellowship on someone else's foundation.

He could certainly express the overall vision for how a gathering of Christians should fit together in their relation to each other, to God, and to all His people. To the Ephesians he wrote:

> *Consequently, you are no longer foreigners and aliens, but fellow citizens with God's people and members of God's household, built on the foundation of the apostles and prophets, with Christ Jesus himself as the chief cornerstone. In him the whole* built fellowship *is joined together and rises to become a holy temple in the Lord. And in him you too are being* built together as a fellowship *to become a dwelling in which God lives by his Spirit.* (Eph. 2:19–22)

Paul had to deal with the inadequacies of any imagery for describing this marvelously complicated thing that is the church of God in Christ. Thus he often used the organic analogy of a body, as in 1 Cor. 12, in addition to the physical analogy of a building. He is not averse to mixing the two metaphors, as he does later to the Ephesians when he talks about the work of leaders "to prepare God's people for works of service, *for the fellowship building of the body of Christ*" (Eph. 4:12). The subtlety of the relationship between growing and building comes out a few verses later:

> *Instead, speaking the truth in love, we will in all things grow up into him who is the Head, that is, Christ. From him the whole body, joined and held together by every supporting ligament, grows and* builds its fellowship *in love, as each part does its work.* (Eph. 4:15–16)

Paul the Contractor

Paul speaks especially like a contractor in his correspondence with the Corinthians. The well-known strain in their fellowship called for a response from its architect that moved beyond big-picture design into directions for practical implementation by those specific people. His two letters to them contain almost all the uses of *oikodomeō* that are usually translated as "edify" or "edification." They refer to pragmatic actions that build people together, that are intended "for building you up rather than pulling you down" (2 Cor. 10:8; cf. 13:10).

Thus the builder responsible for the work of others tells the

Corinthians that everybody may have ideas, but it is love that builds fellowship (1 Cor. 8:1). Everything is permissible for those believers, but not everything builds fellowship; they should seek not their own good but the good of others (10:23). As a contractor, Paul wants to sort out the possible contributions. Thus, since all are eager to have spiritual gifts, they should try to excel in gifts that build fellowship in the church (14:12). He wants them to keep a close eye on the gift of speaking in tongues. Although such a speaker edifies himself, only those who interpret and preach build fellowship in the church (vv. 4–5).

The builder is particularly concerned about bringing newcomers and unbelievers into the fellowship (vv. 22–25). Thus he gives careful instruction for coordinating their public time of worship together: "When you come together, everyone has a hymn, or a word of instruction, a revelation, a tongue or an interpretation. All of these must be done for the *fellowship building* of the church" (v. 26).

The contractor emphasis is perhaps strongest in a long section in which the building theme is implicit in deference to explicit development of the body theme. This is the great teaching in 1 Cor. 12 on the unity of the body amidst diversity of spiritual gifts. Paul recognizes the different kinds of workers: those who speak with wisdom, those with knowledge, those who bring special faith, healing, etc. (vv. 8–11). He reminds them that the working of the Spirit in each is for the common good (v. 7). And he insists that every contribution has an important place in the overall project (vv. 12–26). Add to that his exhortation to the Romans about their specialized functions and the contractor image seems complete: Whatever you are gifted and prepared to do, get on with it (Rom. 12:6–13). We can imagine him impatiently adding: "We have a house to build."

Paul, the Hands-on Builder

Architects are different from contractors in the building business. Both are different from the third and most readily apparent contributor, the workers who actually take material in hand and put the structure together—the carpenters, plumbers, electricians, and other skilled laborers. Carpenters are by far the largest and most general trade and for that reason alone can serve as representative for hands-on builders. Christians have an added reason to feature this image. Our Lord Jesus Christ was a carpenter by trade. He knew the feel and smell of wood and how to join the pieces together. Amid everything else that he did, we can too easily lose sight of the fact that Jesus was a builder in the most elementary sense.

Nor should we forget that Paul of Tarsus was a builder also in the elementary sense of hands-on construction. He earned his living making tents. Such structures were undoubtedly simpler than a house of wood and stones, but they still required construction knowledge. There is evidence that the word *tent*, like *house*, could be used figuratively for home or household.[2] Perhaps this helped give Paul, the tent maker, a special feel for *oikodomeō*.

We have to look to the Acts of the Apostles to see Paul at work with hands-on fellowship building. This level of construction was necessary as he started new churches and had to do the most basic ministries himself. Thus we repeatedly see him as evangelist and preacher in the local synagogue of a city he entered. In Lystra he was healer (Acts 14:8–10). As he went to and from the council meeting in Jerusalem, he strengthened the various churches in the cities through which he passed (14:22; 15:41) and delivered the decisions made at the meeting (16:4). He converted Lydia to begin the church in Philippi and exhorted that house group after being released from prison (v. 40). In Corinth he "devoted himself exclusively to preaching" (18:5). He baptized twelve disciples in Ephesus (19:5). Serving that church for over two years, he taught daily in the lecture hall of Tyrannus (v. 9) and did extraordinary miracles (v. 11). At Troas he celebrated communion and taught late into the night (20:7–11).

On his way to Jerusalem, he returned near Ephesus and called together the elder/leaders that had emerged at that church to bid them farewell. Then he effectively transferred leadership from himself to them, exhorting them to be overseers and shepherds (vv. 25–32). This is the first recorded use of his builder theme as he committed them to the word of God's grace, "which can *build fellowship* and give you an inheritance among all those who are sanctified" (v. 32).

From that time on, Paul was a prisoner at one place or another. His hands-on building days were mostly over. Now his fellowship building would be done from a distance as he functioned

---

[2] J. A. Sanders, *Interpreter's Dictionary of the Bible* (Nashville: Abingdon, 1962), s.v. "tent."

primarily as a contractor, relying on oral and written instructions to the churches and their leaders, who were left to work at building their own fellowship. He had been an architect all along, carrying his vision for fellowship building first in his head and eventually leaving it for posterity in his letters.

Church Leaders as Fellowship Builders Today

Might it ever happen that church leaders would want to put "F.B." (Fellowship Builder) behind their names, as in "the Rev. John Smith, F.B."? Perhaps they would if, out of the many available leadership images in the New Testament, Paul's building analogy provides a helpful self-concept for what church leaders, especially pastors, do. As they use it, they can get clearer direction for their leadership by refining what kind of builder in His kingdom God wants them to be.

Carpenter Ministry

A carpenter minister winds up personally doing most of the work that gets done in a congregation. There may be a carpenter's helper or two and maybe an apprentice, but this leader takes direct personal responsibility for almost any significant contribution to the life of the Christian fellowship.

Who does the teaching, especially among adults, in so many congregations? Who visits the members in the hospital or in their homes? Who makes the evangelism calls or sees that they are made? When the church gathers for worship, who selects the hymns? Who does the praying for a group of gathered members? Who does the counseling?

When the pastor personally does most of these tasks, there is a strong carpenter presence. Congregations learn to expect this kind of ministry and often reinforce it well. Pastors themselves may appreciate this clear set of expectations and the sense of competence that comes from knowing their tasks and doing them well. Like carpenter Frank Casper in the introduction, they can look forward to variety in their work and to going home with a feeling of satisfaction that they have accomplished something important by themselves.

Carpenter ministry is basic. Paul, the premier fellowship builder, did a lot of it. Seminary training for ministry has long emphasized this approach, which remains basic to such fellowship acts as baptism and celebration of the Lord's Supper. Fellowship building involves bringing God's people into closer relationships with God and each other, and pastors can do that well by keeping themselves near the middle of those relationships.

But carpenter ministry is limited in the number and depth of relationships it can support. A carpenter can only do so much work in a day, and one person can be invested in only so many deep relationships. When pastors concentrate on carpentry, their church is likely to remain small or, if it is larger, to have minimal fellowship. Further, while hands-on building can bring stimulating variety, it can also bring frustration, burnout, or guilt to those who are not masters of all the relevant trades. Given that three-quarters of all Protestant churches have fewer than 120 members, carpenter ministry will probably long remain the dominant image for the leadership of building-minded pastors. But there are alternatives that open up more options for fellowship building.

Contractor Ministry

A recently popular pairing of images attributed to Lyle Schaller highlights the difference between carpenter and contractor ministry. A pastor can be a shepherd taking care of a flock, which is the Biblical analogy that readily fits the small congregation today. Or a pastor can be a rancher, leading many shepherds who are out tending the sheep. Like the contractor, the rancher image assumes that others are out doing day-to-day ministry in a congregation. That calls for much different leadership than when one is intent on doing almost everything oneself.

By the way, missionary Paul makes little use of the shepherd image. It appears only in his relationship with the Ephesians, once in his farewell message in Acts 20 and the other in his letter to the congregation when he paired pastors with teachers (Eph. 4:11). Of course, one might well ask how many pastors today have experience with shepherds and sheep ranchers.

Contractors are usually the most dominant factor in housing construction today. When people want a new house, they are likely to deal with a contractor, who may have stepped up to being a developer. A hundred years ago they would probably have talked to a master carpenter, who probably would have done most of the work himself. House building has become much more complicated by the addition of extensive plumbing, electrical wiring and appliances, and sophisticated heating and air-conditioning systems. A tremendous expansion in the variety of available materials has increased the purchasing decisions to be made. The task of getting the right materials and the properly skilled workers together in a timely fashion has put the contractor in the forefront. By any reckoning, building houses is much more expensive today than it was a century ago. Careful management is a natural response.

Contractor ministers will spend much of their time looking for others to do not just the custodial work but real building. They look for teachers to lead not just children's Sunday school classes but an expanding number of adult groups. They develop evangelism teams. They become adept at spotting and guiding care-givers and those with the gift of mercy who can effectively minister to members who are aged, ill, or in distress. They stimulate members to carry out social ministry projects. Some might exercise their function as worship leader while having many members participate in a variety of settings.

On a day-to-day basis, a contractor minister might spend time in meetings, conferences, and telephone calls—not with those who need ministry but with those who are going to offer it. Leading the leaders becomes a specialized ministry of its own. This might mean scouting out resource material for them, writing guidelines, or listening to their personal frustrations and giving encouragement. Formal planning and organizing activities become compelling because there are many workers and they are looking for definition and direction.

It is real "lay ministry" that makes the contractor image possible for pastors. As the apostle Paul believed, every member has something important to contribute. Especially in this century, members themselves have come to believe this is so, even without the support of a theology that recognizes their gifts from the Holy Spirit for that purpose. In a time of rising educational levels, more mobility, and steady social change, fellowship building has become a more complicated and costly effort. This has led to an increased emphasis on the image of the pastor as a managing contractor.

Like contractor Roger Hensley in the introduction, pastors can find themselves functioning like a contractor when building is in their blood and they want to take on more responsibility. There are easier ways to serve the church. But these pastors can have the satisfaction of seeing the widening network of believers joined in lively fellowship through what they do.

Architectural Ministry

Emphasis on the concept of ministry by all the people has been a dominant theme in the discussion of church life in past decades. "Contractor" offers an image for what is already widely accepted in principle among pastors. The architect image and what it represents are relatively new on the scene. It can be seen in the contributions of some of the consultants that churches are increasingly inclined to retain when seeking to improve themselves. Architectural ministry is certainly something to which pastors themselves can aspire.

What does an architect do? Those with "F.A.I.A." behind their names, like Sylvia Pitman, do essentially three things. Two are quite visible, while the third usually rises out of the privacy of their own contemplation.

a. First, they hear and clarify the building users' needs and hopes.

b. Then comes the creative act of fashioning an overall vision for the shape and function of the building.

c. Finally, they make up the detailed construction drawings, or blueprints, to show the other builders what to do.

Hearing and Clarifying

It is a poor architect who meets with a new client and immediately announces what kind of building to build. A successful project requires that the users can live in and carry out their activities in the building as well as admire its attractive appearance. In any significant project the architect will spend considerable time listening to hopes and analyzing the needs that are presented, making suggestions to get feedback from those who have a stake in the outcome and giving rough estimates of the costs for various amounts of square footage. Often architect and client will study other buildings with similar purposes.

While contractor ministers may approach a congregation with a plan well in mind, an architectural minister knows that there are many options for building a fellowship. What finally emerges must fit the believers of that time and place, and it must be something that excites them enough to invest their personal effort and commitment. This early phase may involve committees and other formal planning procedures, or it can be done directly by an astute pastor who spends plenty of time in dialog with a wide range of members. Their strengths, weaknesses, individual and common histories, and perceptions of needs and opportunities all enter the preliminary mix. Like an architect, the pastor has to be competent enough in the structural basics of theology and mission to know what is possible and appropriate within God's purpose for the church. His leadership contribution is to sort this out and to get a sufficient level of agreement to be ready for an overall vision.

Designing the Vision

After absorbing this input, an architect has to bring the expectations, limits, and context together into a design that conveys the vision of what the building will look like when finished. This is the creative act that most clearly separates the good architect from the mediocre. Its product is sketches of the building from various angles and approximate layouts of floor plans. These can become color drawings and even three-dimensional models that place the building in relation to its surroundings. This vision, conveyed as convincingly as possible, lets the clients and users confirm whether the result is what they want and thereby indicate whether they are ready to invest in the vision that will guide the actual construction.

Sometimes church leadership is done with the assumption that no one person should presume to project an overall design for the fellowship, but that the vision should be a compilation of the many different visions held by the members. The leadership theory popular in the human relations/self-actualization movement of previous decades leans this way. But few worthwhile buildings are constructed without an overall coordinated perspective. When they have the talent, pastors are the logical leaders to provide the creative integration that yields a compelling vision for a specific project. They may need the help of an outside consultant, but building design works best when the architect stays involved in the implementation, which is the third step.

A later chapter will explore what an architectural vision for fellowship building might look like. The design involves envisioning people and groups engaged in specific sharing activities, such as worship services with different styles, Bible study or prayer groups with a range of focuses, and social ministry or

37

evangelism teams with particular emphases. The fellowship vision might often include a physical building project to provide appropriate space for the desired interaction. No church vision can be authentic and compelling without a theological interpretation of what God is calling his people to do at that time and place.

Detailing Plans

The last step sets the stage for implementation by many others. An artist's painting displayed on a wall offers only limited help to the builders who are going to join in the project. They need to know specifically where to build the walls, where the windows and doors go, where and how much concrete to pour for the foundation, what kind of plumbing fixtures, lights, and vents to put in and where, how to finish the floor and ceiling, and so on. Blueprints and construction specifications provide this information. If the architect were going to do all the work alone, such drawings might not be necessary; one builder could figure it out and do it at the same time. But when many are involved, the specifications of the overall plan must be thought out first and communicated clearly. All the builders need assurance that the various parts will fit together and meet relevant building codes. By far, most hours of architectural service go into this phase of detailing plans.

A series of stirring sermons setting a vision for a congregation in its response to God's call for the years ahead, as necessary as that is, usually remains far from enough to mobilize members effectively for new fellowship building. They need to know specifically what each can do, given his or her own gifts and circumstances. The leaders who will function as subcontractors will feel more confident when they know how their contribution will fit in and that what they are being asked to do is humanly possible and sensible. Pastors who are going to function as contractors certainly need the communication help of a well-understood plan. At some point detailed descriptions must emerge of what the church's worship, education, witnessing, and service will look like, as well as who will do what by when and how the necessary resources will be found.

But the analogy breaks down when the detailing process is seen as something done by an architectural pastor isolated in an office. Especially in churches, where those who participate are recipients and funders as well as potential workers, there is every reason to have as many heavily involved in this last phase as would ideally be involved in the first. An architectural pastor does not do all the planning any more than a contractor minister does all the hands-on building. That would not be a good use of time for someone with broad spiritual leadership responsibilities, even if one person could lay all the details out for others—which would not be wise, acceptable in many cases, or effective. Functioning as an architect, a pastor will strive to assure that specific planning is done through joint effort and that all the fellowship builders have as much support as they can use.

Assured that the various detailed pictures are in place, a pastor can concentrate on keeping the big picture before everyone. That is the special challenge of the architect analogy for church leaders.

Exploration Topic: Levels of Management and Fellowship Building

In recent years many discussions of church administration have begun with an assumption that modern understandings from business or public administration are the place to start for generating instructive insights for ministers and churches. Perhaps this is exciting for professional managers in church leadership positions, but such presentations are too often of limited help to pastors, whose instincts, mindset, and language are usually different. They often find it hard to make change-producing associations with the pastoral work and the church context they know so well. The images can be hard to fit together.

Scripture seems a more appropriate starting place for ministers and churches. What better model can there be than the apostles Paul and Peter and the early churches they led? The basics of leadership are such that what these church leaders wrote about is not all that different from what modern administrators talk about. It is appropriate for church leaders today to look for helpful leadership insights from the world of modern management—so long as that is done on a foundation of Biblical understandings of purpose and function.

To help us fit together different sets of images, we can relate the church leader images of this chapter to distinctions that business managers are accustomed to making. Their work is usually divided into upper-level, middle-level, and first-level management. Those at each level are leaders of other followers. At the first level, supervisors and foremen have the most direct contact with the workers; they are the hands-on leaders with specific assignments and immediate deadlines. The president and vice presidents at the upper level are usually removed from the day-to-day activity; they concentrate on designing long-range goals and outcomes. The middle-level divisional directors and departmental chiefs think in more limited terms of monthly progress and special projects; they coordinate the first-level leaders. All are builders, striving for something beyond what is at hand.

We might think of the three sets of images this way:

architect	
	upper-level managers
helmsman	

contractor/	
	middle-level managers
steward	

carpenter	
	first-level managers
shepherd	

As we have seen, most pastors think and act like carpenters and shepherds. Because most managers function at the first level, the management which pastors mostly see refects this limited image of leadership.

To the extent that leadership development for pastors is similar to executive development for managers, the direction for improvement lies in learning to think and act according to higher level expectations. That involves broadening perspectives and developing skills to guide the work of others. Pastors will seldom want to think of themselves as CEOs (chief executive officers) of the corporation. But like Paul, they can aspire to be architects for the fellowship under construction. These two roles have much in common. When pastors do not fulfill the church needs for middle and upper level management, then other leaders need to be incorporated into the church leadership structure.

Chapter 3 _____

The Mission: Building
a Lively Spiritual Household

Meet four members of Christ Church. They are some of the building blocks for the fellowship-building efforts of their church leaders, headed by the pastor, William Baumeister.

Al Anderson is a 55-year-old owner of a small shoe store, who has been a member of Christ Church since its founding 30 years ago. He and his wife Betty attend church once or twice a year. He was a church officer 20 years ago. When the pastor visited him two years ago, he talked with pride about "his" church and the window he had contributed in memory of his parents. He occasionally contributes to a special project, if asked.

Chuck Corley is in his late 30s. He and his wife Donna have three children. He is an industrial coatings salesman and has enjoyed his years in the Whitfield Junior Chamber of Commerce. He and Donna joined Christ Church eight years ago when he took a job that brought them to Whitfield. Chuck has been more active in this church than in the previous two they attended. Donna and the children have found a comfortable fit. They are all regulars in Sunday school and Bible class as well as the worship service. Chuck has served on three church committees and now chairs the stewardship committee. He is busy planning the next campaign around a "Pony Express Saddlebag" concept that he saw used in a neighboring congregation. He gets frustrated when other members do not do their share, but his enthusiasm and persistence usually carry enough others along to get the job done on any project that he is leading. Chuck wants the church to grow and is becoming convinced that the congregation should add a director of Christian education. He is already talking about a building expansion for the educational wing.

Barbara Becker is in her early 50s and works as a secretary

41

in a local firm. Her husband died 10 years ago; they had no children. She has been a member of Christ Church for 15 years. It is part of the denomination of her parents and in which she grew up. She has family in the area, bowls for recreation, and is an avid gardener. Barbara attends Sunday worship faithfully, usually alone. Her offerings are regular and somewhat more than modest. For the most part, that is the extent of her church involvement. If she is personally asked to participate in a special congregational emphasis or program, she can be counted on to do the immediate activity, although mostly on a one-time basis. She enjoys the friendship of a small group of women her age with whom she visits after church services. She has high respect for the pastor and speaks well of his ideas.

Dolores Dunlop is a young woman in her late 20s, married to John and mother of two preschoolers. She is a registered nurse with some training in counseling. Since graduating from a Christian college, she has wanted to "make a difference" in caring for the sick and lonely and sees this as a basic mission of the Christian church. President of her high school senior class, she has always been a leader and dreams of organizing other Christians to give care and comfort. Unsatisfied with hospital nursing, she does not anticipate returning to full-time employment until the children are well along in their school years. She and John, a somewhat retiring engineer her age, are relatively new at Christ Church, having left the previous church because they just did not feel that they fit in. She has shared her ideas with the pastor. For now she and John are active in the young couples Bible study group. She also sings in the choir and helps in the nursery when she can.

Anderson, Corley, Becker, and Dunlop are clearly different people. The differences go beyond age, family status, occupation, and the sort of things that will appear on a biographical data form.

There is also a difference in how these differences will be seen by the pastor. As he meets and reflects on each, Bill Baumeister will likely recognize and react to features that differ from what several of his colleagues might highlight. He will like some of these members more than others. In his fellowship-building efforts, he will expect more from some than from others but maybe less than a neighboring pastor might look for. How he thinks these church people got to be the way they are will determine much of his reaction to each.

Other leaders of the church might also differ in how they see and react to members like these four. Their relationships with and attitudes toward each may differ from the pastor's perspective. Part of their reaction may depend on how they see themselves as members. Is Al Anderson a burden to try to ignore or a potential blessing? Chuck Corley is clearly a key member and apparently a fine Christian, but is he a potential rival for leadership, especially if Baumeister is not enthusiastic about adding a director of Christian education? Betty Becker is easy to like. Is she settled into a pattern of participation that will not change? Dolores Dunlop is refreshing in her faith-centered enthusiasm. What will happen with her in a couple of years?

There are many other persons that church leaders will want to see and be concerned about. Some are not members but might eventually join. They could be a John Davidson, who visited church with a friend, or a Bill Brecht, who came to a young adult gathering. Consider them guest participants or interested observers.

Church leaders will also want to think about people like a Sally Smith, who lives down the street but has never stopped by the church, or a Herb Jackson, who drives by the church every day on the way to work and knows only that there is a church on the corner. Call them uninterested observers. Add to these the countless many who do not yet know anything about this church and who remain strangers.

How are these people viewed by the pastor and other church leaders? Do guests and interested observers get noticed? What will happen to them after the first encounter or after several? How much thought in the last year has been given to the people who might have noticed this church but have not taken any initiative to make contact? Will any effort be made to reach out to strangers?

Some Images
from Fellowship-Builder Peter

The apostle Paul gave us the analogy of the church leader as builder, indeed architect. From the apostle Peter we can find

43

a potent analogy for the followers—those "to be built into a spiritual house."

Writing in his first letter to God's elect scattered throughout Asia Minor, Peter, the Rock, tells them to think about themselves this way:

> As you come to him, the living Stone . . . you also, like living stones, are being *built as a fellowship* into a spiritual house to be a holy priesthood, offering spiritual sacrifices acceptable to God through Jesus Christ. (1 Peter 2:4–5)

To be noted first is that Peter knows about fellowship building. He uses the same verb, *oikodomeō*, that Paul favors, and he gives it the same unusual nonphysical meaning. Wanting to convey that meaning most clearly, he adds the almost redundant object, "spiritual house," which his readers would have understood as "household." Thus he says that his readers are being built as a fellowship into a spiritual household. The purpose of this spiritual household of believers alive in Christ is that, having full access to God, all therein may live their lives as a sacrificial response (v. 5), witnessing to God's action in calling them into this new life of light (v. 9). Peter then goes on at great length in the rest of the letter to describe what life should be like in the spiritual household of the people of God.

The key builder analogy in this verse is "like living stones." "Living" and "stone" have to be considered together. "Stone" is not meant to refer to something inanimate, although that possibility might exist, as we shall see. Peter really means the raw material for construction, since stones or manufactured adobe bricks were the primary material for wall construction in those days. Wood had its place, too, pointing to the analogy of carpentry ministry for hands-on fellowship building. This could just as well be called a brick-laying ministry.

The modifier is "living," or "having vitality." Through faith in Christ, the living Stone, believers have true life, and this life from Christ makes them living stones, able to be built together as a spiritual household. The basic point of Peter's analogy is to contrast being full of life in Christ with being dead to God without Christ and thus unsuitable to become part of the spiritual household.

The first step of church leadership for mission is the evangelism work of spreading the Word of salvation that can make hearers come alive in Christ and thus be a part of the spiritual house, the church. Fellowship building has to start with finding the lost and using God's means of grace to deliver them as the raw material for the fellowship life of believers. Basic to the building mission is reaching out with the Gospel and bringing individuals into the community of the people of God.

But the mission is not finished when people become living stones through a church's ministry of Word and Sacrament. That is the start of the mission that Peter highlights. These new stones must now be put together to become a household. The relevant Greek word here is the same *oikos* that, as developed in chapter 2, will be translated here as "fellowship." For the most part, household and fellowship are interchangeable words.

For those already living in Christ, the building material analogy lends itself to further extension, even though Peter probably did not have such alternatives in mind. Other images flow more readily from the adjective "lively," which is used in the King James Version.

Christians involved in fellowship building may be something less than lively, even though there is spiritual life in them. Call them *passive stones*, waiting to be put into place in the household under construction. We can think of *lively stones* as members who do not just wait; they have initiative and look for ways to contribute to the joining together of everybody. Of course, there is always the possibility of *inactive stones*, members who have become so distant from fellowship interaction that their life in the body and perhaps even their life in Christ is to all appearances extinct.

Cornerstone is another alternative. Peter suggests this image by citing Isaiah to describe Christ as a chosen and precious cornerstone. While he does not extend this analogy to believers, we might explore that comparison. If members of the spiritual household can be living stones like *the* living Stone, can not some also be cornerstones like *the* cornerstone?

In ancient construction, the stones set at the corners of the foundation determined the overall size and design of a house. They established where the rest of the building materials would go. The first corner set the location of the house and represented the major decisions and commitment for the project. Houses, of course, had more than one corner, and the most interesting houses that supported a broad and varied range of family functions had many corners. Moving from a simple to a many-cornered house involved complicated design and careful planning to fit walls, floors, and roofs together. The necessary building skill also increased for such projects.

Some members of a fellowship may be cornerstones in the sense of setting a new direction or program for that church. These words from Peter contain a second important follower analogy that simply cannot be overlooked. Peter called the early Christians a "holy priesthood." Verse 5, along with the "royal priesthood" of verse 9, has become, of course, the charter passage for lay ministry. At various ages in the history of the Christian church, the implications of this understanding have been revolutionary for viewing the nature of the church and the ever-present issues of leadership. The followers are not a lower class of members than those ordained into the office of the pastoral ministry instituted by Christ. All stand on an equal footing as priests with direct access to God. Within this priesthood the church calls some of its own to pastoral leadership, but that does not mean that the ability to make major leadership contributions according to their gifts is thereby denied to the rest.

Recognizing and Reacting to Member Building Stones

As fellowship-building leaders look at the members of their congregation, what do they see?

Inactive Stones

Undoubtedly there are some inactive stones, or at least people that the leaders may choose to see and treat as, for all practical purposes, inanimate members who have drifted out of the life of the church. Some might tend to see them as dead stones or tombstones, which they would be only if they no longer have a saving faith in Christ. The term *inactive* leaves the question of their faith open. Is Al Anderson an inactive stone? Maybe. If Bill Baumeister or other leaders put him in that category in their thinking, dislike him for that reason, and treat him as material with little potential, there is a good chance that Al will fulfill those expectations.

Some pastors have been known to see a quarter or even half of their congregation as people who lack a basic spiritual commitment and to feel that the church would be better off without them. Perhaps they are right. But besides depending on their own discriminating perception, that conclusion rests on how they see the basics of faith, the nature of the church, and the challenge of fellowship building.

Passive Stones

Most congregations will appear to have most of their members in the category of passive stones. These people are not at the fringe and may indeed be quite faithful in the central fellowship activity of joint worship. Their chief characteristic is minimal involvement in life beyond one activity or so; they might do something else when asked, but with an air of hesitance or reluctance. They tend to be more receivers than givers of support.

Barbara Becker is a passive stone. Her faith, her church, and her pastor are important to her. She is certainly part of the fellowship. But she has given little thought to how she might contribute to the fellowship beyond her Sunday presence and her offering.

What is the fellowship-building challenge with passive stones? That depends on how the builder sees them. They can remain as objects of ministry and the basic reason for a congregation's existence. In traditional churches they are the laity before the rediscovery of lay ministry. Traditional pastors can readily appreciate their complacency as they find their place and tend to stay there. Indeed, carpenter (or brick-laying) pastors and passive stones usually get along quite well.

Even from the viewpoint of ambitious fellowship building, some members will always be passive stones. By personality and with the gifts they have received from the Holy Spirit, they may be functioning to their fullest extent. But many will have the potential to move further in the direction of giving support to others as well as receiving it from them. Ministry that can pull this out of them will seek to shape their expectations and arrange opportunities to which they can respond. That is a topic for the next chapter.

Lively Stones

Every believer in Christ has life in Him and therefore is a living stone. But in this analogy "lively stone" is used to describe those members of the fellowship whose participation is characterized by perceptible energy, initiative, and active readiness to serve others. These are the doers in a congregation—in the common reckoning, the one-third who carry the other two-thirds of the members. Some will be leaders, stimulating and organizing the contributions of others. Some will be workers, showing up often to prepare the altar for worship, repair broken tables, teach Sunday school, cook meals, visit the sick, stuff envelopes, make stewardship calls, usher, or do any of the wide range of activities that turn a church into a lively congregation. They will not necessarily do their activity within the church building. It can also be an action that extends the fellowship into the community.

Chuck Corley is a lively stone. He bubbles with energy ready to be harnessed for the good of the fellowship. He will also be a leader wherever he invests himself. Like many lively stones, he represents a challenge to fellowship builders to sustain his interest in their congregation and to guide his leadership contributions. How will Pastor Baumeister respond to him?

Lively stones are the raw material for contractor ministry. At an elementary level, contractor builders could regard them mostly as helpers to expand the coverage of simple tasks. Experienced contractors would keep an eye out for skilled workers who can assume increasing responsibility for ministry functions that pastors themselves have been accustomed to doing. Undoubtedly there are people waiting to be seen and treated as subcontractors, taking administrative responsibility and accountability for major areas of the church's fellowship life.

Cornerstones

Cornerstones are not to be confused with pillars, which church people are accustomed to respecting in their midst. By their longevity, faithfulness, hard work, or perhaps financial support, pillars come to be depended on to provide basic stability and support for a congregation.

Cornerstones in this analogy help design the shared life of a fellowship. Pillars may be key and lively stones, but cornerstones function at the foundation level of shaping the continued growth of a church, presenting new angles that carry the work of others in new directions. Their chief contributions are ideas that they can turn into programs to attract the willing participation of many others.

Cornerstone contributions border on architectural ministry.

In this respect they touch on the special contribution of a professional worker in the church. Indeed, in most congregations the paid staff, called and expected by the church to take program responsibility, will most likely be the cornerstones. The challenge in multiple-staff ministries is to let each person contribute to the design. Senior pastors sometimes have difficulty with staff leadership because they want to remain the only cornerstone, relegating the work of others to contractor ministry at best. But congregations realize more of their potential when they have many cornerstones—assuming that the chief architect can keep all these initiatives fitted into a coherent design.

Dolores Dunlop is ready to be a cornerstone. She comes gifted with ideas, skill, and commitment, and she seems available to take leadership responsibility. What she could contribute in the area of a diaconate ministry of care and service is not just her own personal care-giving but perhaps a whole new program that would involve dozens of others in a basic fellowship function. With her, Christ Church could turn a corner in ministry. But at this time she is far from being a pillar of the congregation. She is new, young, a woman, not on the staff, and without a constituency. Some might feel that she first needs to prove herself through the time-honored ways that young mothers enter the life of the fellowship. But she could also be helped to voice her special vision and be given the backing necessary to gain attention from leaders in the church. Depending on how Pastor Baumeister reacts to her, in three years she could be heading an exciting fellowship ministry, or she and her family could be gone to look for another church more ready to put her gifts to work.

Everyone knows that there are differences among the members of a church. Less evident are the differences among leaders in how those member differences are recognized and treated. Fellowship building advances as church leaders become more discerning in spotting this potential and more confident in guiding that potential into a constructive contribution to the overall vision.

The Leadership Mission: Moving the Building Blocks

To watch a house being built is to watch movement. Heavy equipment moves the earth in preparation for a foundation. There is steady movement in the delivery of materials, but the real building takes place once they are at hand. Masons carry concrete blocks off the big pile and assemble them one by one into a foundation wall. Carpenters pick two-by-fours and two-by-tens off their piles, hoist them where they are needed, and fit them together. Plumbers move pipes and electricians pull wires. A house cannot be built without the movement of materials. People are the building material of churches. This is the point of Peter's analogy of the living stones built into a spiritual house. To build fellowship means that something is going to happen to the people who will be involved in the project. They are going to be moved— first so that they come into the building project by becoming members of a congregation and then so that they fit together better in the congregation—so that they become more of the church God is calling them to be.

The movement that should happen is the general topic of the next chapters. We cannot outline in detail how people should be brought into a congregation or where each church member should be fitted. That is a determination to be made at the job site through careful deliberation about those to be reached and with each member about personal and church needs and aspirations. Building with an architect's skill is not done with one blueprint that fits all.

The general direction of movement for fellowship building can be identified here, however. It is suggested in the following diagram:

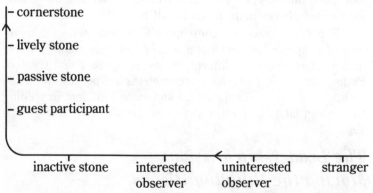

Two basic convictions are necessary to make the fellowship-building theme compelling for church leadership. Both involve

50

movement. One defines the leader task as moving people inward into believing participation in a Christian fellowship. The other projects movement upward toward more lively levels of fellowship involvement in a church.

Movement Inward

The first conviction is fundamental to the basic identity of church and its leaders: *Being in the church and in a congregation is better than being outside.* Understanding *the* church as the whole body of all believers, this means that church leaders really believe that a person is better off as a saved follower of Christ than being unsaved. Without that motive there is not much reason to take the Christian church seriously.

But wanting to move people *inward also means* believing that a Christian is better off participating in the life of a church—a congregation—than remaining in isolation from other believers. This is a conviction that goes beyond wanting someone to be saved. It includes recognition that God calls and expects his children to gather together (congregate) as church. The assumption that people should move inward involves truly believing that life in a congregation, a Christian fellowship, is good for believers and that they can be brought to appreciate this form of blessing from God.

The diagram shows several stages of movement inward into a fellowship. Starting with the great number of unchurched strangers to a particular congregation, the challenge is to make some of them familiar with this church, even though they remain uninterested observers. Of course, some can be helped to become interested observers who still do not participate in the fellowship. Getting some of them to interact with others in the fellowship, that is, to participate in some form of church life, is the key step that shifts the direction from inward to upward.

Movement of people who are not yet members through the various stages of awareness of a congregation and its offerings is a process that continually happens, even though church leaders typically have little understanding of how. Marketing can be a helpful management discipline for increasing understanding of this process, which does not yet necessarily involve distinctly Christian dynamics. Some insights are offered in Exploration Topic A of chapter 5.

Of course, true involvement in congregational fellowship life

51

cannot happen for a person who has not yet been brought to faith in Christ. Movement inward is fundamentally the work of evangelistic outreach. Commitment to movement inwards implies that churches should grow in numbers.

Movement Upward

The second conviction for making fellowship building a compelling leadership mission is that *more Christ-centered fellowship interaction is better than less.* A congregation with lively fellowship life is a better and more effective church than one with mostly shallow fellowship life and certainly better than one with nonexistent fellowship life. Making that assumption more convincing is one of the purposes for the discussions that follow. The author of Hebrews writes: "Let us consider how we may spur one another on toward love and good deeds. Let us not give up meeting together, as some are in the habit of doing, but let us encourage one another."

This position will only become a compelling belief when fellowship is understood as a much broader interaction encompassing personal and church life than the merely social times of togetherness that usually carry that label now. This does not mean that a congregation without lively fellowship is no longer a real church. It is a church, but one in need of being built up. It is a church in need of leadership.

Lively fellowship is already an application of the lively stone image. It happens when many lively stones are built together. Just as we can distinguish different kinds of building stones, so we can recognize different kinds of fellowship life. In fact, fellowship life can be practically nonexistent; that would happen in a church with mostly inactive building stones. Some churches function for all practical purposes at the level of *inactive fellowship life.* This can happen when the financial means exist to continue an institutional presence with virtually no response. While faith, rather than good works, determines whether a group of people constitute a church, if there is no evidence of faith or a desire to express it, the church is as good as dead.

The real alternative to lively fellowship is a *shallow fellowship life.* It happens when believers have little interaction with each other and find little to share. Sunday morning worship is the extent of participation for most, and that may be sporadic. Shallow fellowship tends to be the result of a preponderance of passive stones. These are the believers who are hesitant or reluctant to become involved with others. Church is a part of their life, but they keep that part narrowly defined.

The steps for movement upward are derived from recognition of the different kinds of building blocks present in a congregation. Inactive stones, who may still be believers, need to be brought back into church participation. Guest participants should be brought to the point of being a real building stone, that is, a Christian knowingly committed to the body of Christ present in that congregation. Among those Christians visibly involved in church life, the building challenge is to move passive stones to become lively stones. An extra challenge is to help some lively stones become cornerstones. Developing these dynamics is basic to church leadership for mission. How to stimulate this movement is the subject of chapters 4 and 5.

These categories and definitions are of course much oversimplified and suggest general directions. Exceptions will abound. But something like the overall direction suggested here is what turns church leadership into ministry and makes this ministry a necessary and exciting mission.

A Pastoral Qualifier

If Peter had not suggested it, the analogy of believers as building material for churches would perhaps seem rather crass to a sensitive pastor. It undoubtedly can be used badly, especially when people are manipulated merely as a means to some grand plan that a building-minded leader imposes on a congregation. If they are raw material, it is ultimately for development by their Creator and Savior, not just by leaders who want their church to look good. Peter does help clarify that as believers come to *the* living stone, Christ, they are being built into a spiritual house.

The analogy of stones for house building has several other potential weaknesses. It emphasizes the movement between stones, fitting them together. But of course there is movement within each stone. Believers are continually moving in their personal lives as their age, relationships, needs, and spiritual vitality change. Ministry has to stay attuned to serving them where they are in their lives, even when that changes. But one dares to hope that a rich fellowship life will facilitate such response by many others as well as by the pastor.

House building as an analogy suggests that the building project has an end. Once put in place, blocks, lumber, and pipes tend to stay in place and the project is finished. But fellowship building is done with people who change and move out of place. The spiritual house is always under construction. Church leaders should never rest content that their building job is done, and the analogy is misleading if it leaves such an impression. Building without finishing can be frustrating. But if the job were ever done, leadership would lose its excitement and mission.

There are always building blocks to be moved inward and upward in Christ's church. How to get better at this is the subject of the next chapter.

Exploration Topic: Perception and Management Development

Recognizing differences among church people is part of refining a leader's perceptions. Getting perceptions clarified and awareness refined is the best way to start the process of becoming a better leader. That is why the formal study of management and organizational behavior usually starts with a discussion of the perception process and how it shapes response. Managers can only respond to what they see, and they can respond better when they see more.

Recognizing—and labeling—differences in how followers are seen is the fundamental contribution of one of the earliest and most popular management theorists. Douglas McGregor gave the literature the categories of Theory X and Theory Y. He used theory in its etymologically correct sense of a way of looking at something. Developing management theory in the 1950s, he noted that assumptions about human work behavior prevalent in previous decades no long seemed to fit then-current management challenges. He called for a change in perception. The son of a Presbyterian minister, he presented a perspective that has a theological tone in its understanding of human nature.[1]

With a *Theory X* perspective, managers are prone to assume that human beings have an inherent dislike of work. They see their management task as controlling and directing workers and threatening them with punishment to get them to put forth adequate work effort. From this viewpoint managers see the av-

---

[1] Douglas McGregor, *The Human Side of Enterprise* (McGraw Hill, 1960), 33–34.

erage worker as wanting this kind of controlling leadership. There is a rough parallel between Theory X in management and the passive stones that many ministers are prone to see when they think about average church members. The leadership job then becomes mostly a matter of providing the right kind of control and perhaps even coercion to keep the members functioning in church.

The newer *Theory Y*, according to McGregor, urges the recognition that for most people the expenditure of physical and mental effort in work is as natural as play and rest. People will exercise self-direction and self-control in the service of objectives to which they are committed, and such commitment is a function of the rewards associated with their achievement. Under proper conditions, the average human being learns not only to accept but to seek responsibility.

Lively stones are a rough parallel to the worker envisioned in Theory Y. Participation in fellowship life is something they will want to do as they live out the commitment of their new life in Christ. The challenge is to present specific church-work objectives to which they can commit themselves and experience the rewards of achievement. Church leaders can learn to see that many members will seek responsibility under proper circumstances.

X and Y beg a Z. A *Theory Z* entered management literature in the 1980s through the work of William Ouchi. Reflecting on Japanese management, he used it to describe an organizational context in which workers are encouraged to participate in the development of objectives and the means for achieving them—in effect, to design the job for themselves and others. While theorizing at a different level from McGregor, Ouchi and his Theory Z carry responsible corporate-oriented participation a step farther in shared interaction.[2]

Cornerstones fit roughly within a Theory Z perspective that moves beyond concentrating on lively stones acting within someone else's design. The challenge is to develop a church organizational context in which those special contributions can be recognized and given support to develop.

Managers learning Theory X and Theory Y often conclude that they should take one or the other as the sole guide for their

---

[2] William G. Ouchi, *Theory Z* (Avon Books, 1981).

work. With experience, however, comes recognition that, for all practical purposes, some workers really do fit Theory X assumptions while others fit well within Theory Y expectations. Refining perceptions permits a manager to react more effectively to the given workers and situation at hand. Good theory allows more to be seen at any one time and place.

Chapter 4 _____

The Push and Pull of Moving Christians

Consider this simple image of movement:

a. ————>
   Push

b.   ————>
              Pull

a. To push: to exert force against a thing so as to move it away from where it is.

   to drive, compel, or prod

b. To pull: to exert force so as to move a thing toward the source of the force

   to draw, attract, or tug

Now insert a box to represent an inanimate building block:

It has no active force of its own. It will move only as a builder supplies force. Where that comes from makes little difference, except to the builder.

a. —→☐ Pushing generally lets the muscles apply more force but the direction is harder to maintain.

b. ☐—→ Pulling maintains the direction but with less force.

Now let the box represent a human building block:

A living thing has energy of its own and can move itself. Where the outside influence comes from makes a difference to the person, and therefore to the builder.

a. Pushing drives from behind, is poorly seen, and usually compels the person's motion in any convenient direction that escapes the force, whether or not that is where the builder was aiming.

b. Pulling draws from ahead, usually maintains personal contact, and can attract a person to move toward a specific place, even when that may not be where the person was first going.

Pushing treats human building blocks like resisters and can turn builders into bulldozer drivers.

Pulling can turn building blocks into followers and makes builders into leaders.

Church leaders often feel like drivers, but their bulldozer is not very big or powerful. They want to push programs, and to do that they feel that they must push people. Often the members are not exactly resisting, but they are not charging ahead and serving the Lord with gladness. Where effort by others is really important, the urge to prod them with Law, however gently, is strong.

The bottom-line message of this chapter is: *Don't do that.* More specifically, do not regard church members as building blocks that have to be pushed into place. They need to be pulled. More specifically, *the way to get them into motion is to draw or attract their energy toward the action of interest.* They have energy provided by God through the Gospel. Pulling them means encouraging, stimulating, exciting, and motivating them by finding ways to convey the meaning and power of God's grace.

To say that people cannot be pushed is not to say that no push is involved. Significant action flows out of a powerful push. But that has to come *from within* the person, *not* from behind. Strong motivation is the usual term for this sort of push. Exploration Topics A and C in this chapter will offer guidance for assessing the *push from within* of Christians.

The push/pull distinction is an oversimplified way of introducing the highly complex topic of motivation and how to deal with it as a leader. Add the special dimension that church leaders are dealing with the motivation of *Christians*, and the matter gets incredibly complex. Simplified distinctions become almost a prerequisite for improving the leadership a minister wants to offer.

Program Pull for Internal Pushes

When it comes to moving people in a desired direction, managers in secular organizations are taught to look for and to respond to the motives that can be found among workers. A basic assumption is that a manager really cannot motivate anybody. Popularly, someone might be called a good motivator, as if a coach or supervisor "gave" motivation to others. But technically, motivation is not something that can be given to someone else. It arises from within an individual according to needs unique to each person. The person will move in a direction that promises to fill a need. Presented with an opportunity to find some satisfaction for a need, a worker will be "motivated" to perform. According to this view of management, an effective leader moves people by doing two things: recognizing needs of individuals or groups and arranging opportunities to satisfy those needs. A coach stimulates fresh energy from a team by casting victory as a way to gain respect; a supervisor raises departmental performance by arranging more direct financial rewards.

The image of a path towards a goal provides a framework for this understanding of motivation. According to path-goal analysis (also called expectancy theory), the leader's task is to identify the personal goals on which workers are focusing, even if somewhat unconsciously, and to figure out a path that will help them arrive at one or several of those goals. The challenge is to lay out the path so that their performance will meet organizational goals at the same time. Improvement comes as individuals become more confident that the increased effort or participation will actually bring a higher level of performance and that the desired performance will actually bring results that satisfy personal needs. Of course, from a manager's viewpoint improvement also includes better accomplishment of organizational goals through the higher level of individual performances.

This sort of need-based, path-goal approach is not enough for leadership in a Christian congregation. But it can be helpful for one part of the task: arranging opportunities for personal participation that pull people into action in one or another phase of church life. "Program development" is the usual name for this aspect of church leadership. Much of the administrative work of church leaders revolves around doing programs, and ineffectiveness in this function is a major cause of frustration in congregations and especially among pastors.

Suppose that increased Bible study through a widening network of small groups is an important vision that a fellowship-building pastor holds out for a congregation. The need for more Bible study is hardly controversial, and most believers would acknowledge that they should do more of it. But it is a long way from such a starting point to an established program of 100 people growing in Christ by regularly and gladly studying Scripture in eight home-based groups, with several new ones added each year.

59

That can be seen as a path along which members and friends are "pulled" step by step. Whatever the church's stated goals may be, each individual will consider taking those steps in the light of how participation will help him or her advance toward a personal goal related to fulfilling a perceived need.

A church leader trying to develop this program will first want, much like a manager, to recognize the needs that are present among those who might become involved. Some may be looking for ways to expand their knowledge of Scripture. Most probably have vague hopes that God's Word can help them cope with problems they are facing. Many undoubtedly are looking for meaningful interaction and discussion with other Christians at more than a superficial level. Several other clusters of needs might also be recognized, although these are the most common among small-group Bible study participants.

The program developer's next challenge is to arrange convenient opportunities for members and others to act on these personal needs and to find fulfillment. Will there be a group at a convenient time and place, among people with whom they are comfortable? If they come, will they actually be drawn into Scripture, or will the event be arranged in a way that does not get their attention? If they participate, will they feel that they actually received some help with concerns on their mind, and will they experience a closer relationship with other searchers for Christian meaning in life? To the extent that the offered opportunities are accessible and actually deliver what people are looking for, participation will continue and expand. Then leaders will have "pulled" fellow Christians into the action they set as a church goal.

Seldom will one program meet all possible personal needs and expectations in an area of church life. Those looking for in-depth scholarly Bible study may conclude that small sharing groups do not meet their need. That might call for arranging another program with a different type of Bible study. Effective program development usually involves laying out several paths toward personal goal fulfillment rather than just one.

An average congregation today probably has at least a dozen programs underway at any given time, pulling members into action in the worship, education, service, and witnessing areas of church life. If carefully distinguished, they might number dozens more in many churches. There is no lack of options for packaged programs offered by denomination offices, publishers, or church leaders ready to share what has worked for them.

Carpenter pastors may simply want to take a program conveniently at hand and follow the instructions for implementing it. The results are often encouraging. Frequent failures, however, should raise questions about what went wrong in that particular congregation and why. Architectural pastors will want to ask questions before investing their own and the church's effort in such a visible undertaking. To assure a good fit between needs and purpose, they will often design their own programs.

Knowing what questions to ask is a leadership skill basic to assessing and designing programs. Those questions become more apparent by distinguishing between the push and pull of moving Christians into action. They are part of discovering the internal pushes present among those to be moved and the opportunities that will pull them into action.

Exploration Topic B in this chapter offers guidance for assessing the push by presenting insights from the study of motivational psychology. The next chapter provides a framework for designing the pull by using a model of "Seekers" becoming "Finders." The conceptual framework used in the discipline of marketing can be helpful, as explored in a separate topic in that chapter. It is always necessary to approach these insights with full appreciation for the uniqueness of Christian motivation in church life, discussed in this Exploration Topic A: The Special Self-Push of Christians and Exploration Topic C: Looking for the Holy Spirit.

The Pastor as Preacher and Administrator

As noted earlier, the need-based, path-goal approach to pulling is not enough for the leadership that a pastor should provide. Usually the only strategy available in secular organizations, it is only one possibility for moving Christians in churches. Pastors cannot be content with just accepting and reacting to whatever motives people bring with them into church life. Their special calling is to do something about changing and shaping those motives.

As preacher, the pastor's leadership role is to present convincingly the means through which God moves or "pushes" people—His Word. A Christian's central encounter with God should affect the motives that shape his or her life. Unlike secular leaders, the pastor brings to the motivation process the Word of God, which really can touch people and change their lives. Through the delivered Word, God sends His Spirit to bring people to faith and to energize those who accept His promise of a new life in Christ. In God's church there is plenty of special energy ready to be engaged in action.

As administrator, the pastor's leadership role is to arrange the opportunities for expressing the motives that people bring to church life. Certainly those include motives changed by encounters with Christ. Logically, the right sequence is preaching the life-changing Word followed by administering the programs that express those changes. In such a case, church administration would be an enterprise fundamentally different from other administrative effort. In actuality, program development often brings members as well as others into opportunities to hear the Word and to experience its effects. By first recognizing and reacting to people where they are, church leaders as administrators share much in common with other administrative leaders.

Pastors thus can take a two-strategy approach toward church leadership. As preachers, they concentrate on presenting the God-given means that affect the internal push of the individual. As administrators, they concentrate on arranging the pull into action. If a choice has to be made, the Word-presenting function is, of course, the more basic. But a choice does not have to be made. Pursuing both strategies is the challenge of faithful ministry in God's church.

A single-strategy ministry will yield something less than fully effective church leadership. In God's kingdom, faith without works is dead, and that can happen if only the first strategy is pursued. But in addition to being worthless before God, church works without faith will not last long, and that can happen when the administrative strategy alone is used. The two approaches belong together in the push and pull of leading Christians.

Exploration Topic A:
The Special Self-Push of Christians
The Ideal

Preachers have little difficulty identifying the special push that Christians should bring to their life together—or at least

62

describing what the ideal should look like. The apostle Paul gives us much-beloved words and images for that purpose. To cite one example:

> *Since, then, you have been raised with Christ, set your hearts on things above . . . not on earthly things. For you died, and your life is now hidden with Christ in God. . . . Put to death, therefore, whatever belongs to your earthly nature: sexual immorality, impurity, lust, evil desires and greed. . . . You used to walk in these ways, in the life you once lived. But now you must rid yourself of all such things. . . . Do not lie to each other, since you have taken off your old self with its practices and have put on the new self, which is being renewed in knowledge in the image of its Creator. (Col. 3:1–10)*

As a result of new life in Christ, this is what life in his body should look like:

> *Therefore, as God's chosen people, holy and dearly loved, clothe yourselves with compassion, kindness, humility, gentleness and patience. Bear with each other. . . . Forgive as the Lord forgave you. And over all these virtues put on love, which binds them all together in perfect unity. Let the peace of Christ rule in your hearts, since as members of one body you were called to peace. And be thankful. Let the word of Christ dwell in you richly as you teach and admonish one another with all wisdom, and as you sing psalms, hymns and spiritual songs with gratitude in your hearts to God. And whatever you do, whether in word or deed, do it all in the name of the Lord Jesus, giving thanks to God the Father through him. (vv. 12–17)*

For the Colossians, Paul describes the ideal as a people of God with a new nature from Christ at peace with each other and living good moral lives. This is certainly the theological foundation for church life.

But the Colossian passages read like a prescription for a *gentle* fellowship rather than a *lively* fellowship. Is there more to the ideal than peacefulness flowing from a love that forgives and forbears? Where is the push that produces the inventive initiatives of outreach to others and moves a congregation beyond gentleness to liveliness? For the Galatians, Paul adds this component:

> *You, my brothers, were called to be free. But do not use your freedom to indulge the sinful nature; rather, serve one*

another in love. The entire law is summed up in a single command: "Love your neighbor as yourself." (Gal. 5:13–14)

The new image is slavery, enslaving oneself to another—an act of love that is often translated as serving one another. For the Corinthians, Paul explains that this love goes so far as to put the interests of others ahead of your own (1 Cor. 10:23). What such a push for fellowship interaction could look like is found in the description of the first Christian fellowship that lived the ideal, at least for a while. After Pentecost, "all the believers were together and had everything in common. Selling their possessions and goods, they gave to anyone as he had need" (Acts 2:44–45).

The Reality

Fellowship-builder Paul knew the reality as well as the ideal. Tactfully, he used himself as an example:

> *We know that the law is spiritual; but I am unspiritual, sold as a slave to sin. I do not understand what I do. For what I want to do I do not do, but what I hate I do. And if I do what I do not want to do, I agree that the law is good. As it is, it is no longer I myself who do it, but it is sin living in me. I know that nothing good lives in me, that is, in my sinful nature. For I have the desire to do what is good, but I cannot carry it out. For what I do is not the good I want to do; no, the evil I do not want to do—this I keep on doing. (Rom. 7:14–19)*

Paul knew well the inner push of believers who live in Christ now, but not yet fully. Before God takes us to the next world, we have here only the beginnings, not the completed new life: "We ourselves, who have the first fruits of the Spirit, groan inwardly as we wait eagerly for our adoption as sons, the redemption of our bodies" (8:23).

Martin Luther gave a wonderful image for understanding what it means to live a new life (Rom 6:4) at the same time that we live in our old nature. In describing how to see God at work in baptism, he says, "This signifies that the Old Adam should, by daily contrition and repentance, be drowned and die with all sins and evil lusts and, again, a new person daily come forth and arise, who shall live before God in righteousness and purity forever" (The Small Catechism, Article IV of the Sacrament of Baptism).

The image is one of *daily* drowning out the old and letting the new come forth. When in God's grace we realize some of the new today, we can still expect to have to drown out the old again tomorrow. Inevitably, the leadership of fellowship life has to concentrate on the new life and the old as they co-exist.

Dealing with the Reality

The dual nature of believers—the new being embedded in the old—is what makes ministry so challenging and so complicated. It is naive to approach church life only as the ideal. Two specialties of pastoral ministry have to confront this complexity most directly: pastoral counseling and pastoral administration.

In one-on-one counseling, the pastor hears many individual variations of the story of how a believer's motivation gets mixed and confused. Simply to reiterate what a Christian's behavior should be often does little to change or straighten out what actually is. Simply to label as sin what does not seem to fit can be an uncompassionate oversimplification. Helpful insights come from an improved understanding of the drives or motives that lie behind behaviors. These can be God-created but poorly directed; they may or may not be sinful. The study of psychology has produced considerable insight for pastors to apply in such counseling. It presents a variety of models or theories that can suggest what to look for when trying to understand the inner push.

Administration can be regarded as an extension of counseling, but with dozens and hundreds of people instead of one or three. The common point is perceiving and reacting to the needs and drives that shape their personal and interpersonal behavior. With such perception a pastoral counselor is able to help individuals find their freedom in the Gospel to act out their God-given inner push, as well as to help them gain confidence to refrain from irresponsible behavior in doing so. With such a sense of personal needs, a pastoral administrator can help members of a fellowship express their impulses to live a new life as they arise in various forms. At the same time, such leadership can develop shared expectations to help them curb the effects of the old nature, which remains constantly with them. These reminders often take the form of the many policies, rules, and even penalties that are so familiar in life in organized communities.

As preacher of the Word of God, a pastor is privileged to work with the means that generate again and again the push of the new life in Christ. As administrator of fellowship life, a pastor can work on the pull of opportunities for action that satisfy the drives a Christian brings to church life. As both preacher and administrator, a pastor shapes expectations for shared life in Christ by sending messages that both expand believers' intentions and discourage what the believers, at their best, do not want to do.

Developing expectations shared with others to help curb the old nature can be seen as applications of the Law—God's expectations. Of course church leaders have always had to deal with the reality of believers stuck in behaviors less than the ideal.

To aid in pastoral leadership for Christian living, classical Protestant theologians distinguished between three uses of the Law—the Law in which Paul could delight in his inner being (Rom. 7:22). The first is as a mirror to bring recognition and repentance for failing God's full demands of his people. This is the prerequisite for the daily regeneration that comes from receiving again the Gospel message of God's forgiveness and acceptance. The second is to curb the ever-present impulses that push away from God-pleasing life. These are the messages with negative content and consequences for acts that Christians should check and refrain from in their lives together. The third is to teach and guide renewed believers in what God would have them do. These are the positive messages of what ideal Christian behavior should be.

Church administration deals with both the second and third uses of the Law. The rules, procedures, and prescribed relationships of administration do need to be in place to constrain selfish behavior that would harm others, especially those in the fellowship. Development of organizational goals is an important way to identify and guide corporate Christian behavior for the fellowship. But administration alone, like Law, will not build lively fellowship life. This happens by concentrating on the repentance-induced, Gospel-generated inner push, without which Christian fellowship life cannot be sustained.

Exploration Topic B: Motivational Psychology

Like counselors, administrative fellowship builders can gain insights from understanding the needs of those they would lead by looking at models and theories from the study of psychology. Unlike counselors, who typically dip into abnormal psychology, fellowship leaders will want to look mostly at motivational psychology. Here the objective is to understand and react to the normal behavior of relatively normal people.

Whether Christians are to be considered normal people like others in society can be a theological issue. But extensive empirical observation, both scientific and informal, suggests that the needs and drives of renewed church people look much like those of everyone else whom God created in this world. The difference may be in how these needs and drives are expressed.

The Basic Model

The basic and most popular psychological model looks at motivation as a process that can be distinguished in several steps. Six are considered here. Motivation begins when a need triggers a drive or motive to search for ways to satisfy that need. This drive then stimulates behavior that is directed at a goal, the achievement of which is perceived as most likely to bring satisfaction and reduce the need. The steps can be diagramed this way:[1]

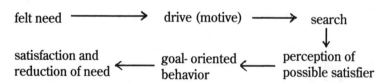

The source of needs and what kinds there are remain basic questions. Typologies are easier to make than explanations, and some typologies will be offered here. Needs begin with a state of deprivation that emerges within a person, such as lacking sufficient bodily nourishment or rest. But insufficiency is not a need until it is recognized. Needs that are identified by someone else may not be felt enough by an individual to begin a motivation cycle. This is important for ministers to recognize. They often tend to project needs that are not self-generated onto other people. Such needs are identified in relation to some standard set forth by the church, such as the need for a person to hear the

---

[1] This summary is from Arthur G. Bedeian and William F. Glueck, *Management* (Dryden Press, 1983), p. 135.

Gospel. That need may exist, but it does not generate specific behavior until a person feels it enough to arouse a drive. Church people have two vocabularies of need. The one that is most helpful for understanding general motivation is the felt need of the person whose behavior is the focus of attention.

The drive is the energy aroused by the inner tension emerging from the need and making it felt. This is the movement, or motive, that becomes action. It turns a need into a want. An example is hunger. The strength of the drive or motive depends on how much in need a person feels.

While one person can contribute to the felt need of another by depriving him or her of something, ordinarily others can only respond to the wants of a person to whom they are relating. They can do this by intervening in the rest of the motivation cycle to present alternative ways to fill a want that the person may not have known about (such as a new restaurant), to modify the motivated person's perception of how the alternatives can supply what is wanted, thus making a specific alternative more attractive (highlighting a specialty featured by the restaurant), to show which behavior (such as going into the restaurant) can accomplish the goal that the person has chosen as most likely to fill the need (eating the meal and satisfying the hunger). Actual satisfaction is the result of a cycle that avoids frustration and yields behavior likely to be repeated in the future.

These contributions to the secondary steps become part of the "pulling" process, leading people into behavior desired in the fellowship life of Christians. Such leadership helps individuals in their search, perception, identification of specific behaviors, and achievement of satisfaction. In short, this can be called "delivering satisfaction." But again, the pull can only be effective when there is a push, originating in an individual's inner drive triggered by a need.

Recognizing Needs

There are dozens of models for categorizing and describing human needs. The one by psychologist Abraham Maslow is most popular in management development, largely for its simplicity. He suggests that five types of need motivate most observable behavior.[2]

---

[2] Abraham Maslow, *Motivation and Personality* (New York: Harper, 1954).

Bodily needs are those that result from deprivations that the body experiences, such as the need for food, air, or rest. When felt, these needs can displace attention from other needs.

Security needs arise from threats to physical safety and also to familiar patterns of routine living. The need for stability and predictability in relationships and anticipations of the future can produce strong preservation drives in the face of change, something that church leaders with new ideas must continually recognize.

Affiliation needs are for closeness to others, as expressed in reaching out for acceptance, affection, and friendship. The prospect of being alone shapes much of the motivation for interacting with others. In churches the urge to move closer to God also yields the urge to share the experience with others and becomes a basis of fellowship.

Esteem needs are for distance or distinctiveness from others and can be sought as recognition, respect (being well regarded), or standing before others, called "status." Surrounded by others, a person's concern for loss of individuality can motivate a variety of efforts to be different. The need for distinctiveness over against the unchurched is a fundamental drive for church fellowship, which also has to reckon with needs for status within the fellowship.

Self-actualization needs are for feelings of fulfillment, achievement, or the realization of one's perceived potential. They often emerge from fear of loss of purpose in life. While being concerned about purpose, churches must recognize the need for unique self-fulfillment that each individual can have.

Maslow posits that these needs stand in a hierarchy from lower (primary) to higher (secondary). Bodily and security needs are basic, and the theory holds that other needs will not motivate much behavior until the primary ones are fairly well satisfied. Evidence for this view has not been convincing and is even less clear in church life—except perhaps in the area of security. Ministers readily exchange stories of resistance to change among church people, even when attractive offerings for "higher level" needs are made. The theory offers a rationale.

Part of the appeal of Maslow's model to managers is the suggestion that among American workers today, in general, primary needs are satisfied well enough that they are no longer strong motivators for new behaviors. Therefore, incentives or offers of need-satisfying rewards should be focused on the affiliation, esteem, and self-actualization needs.

David McClelland expands on these secondary types with a model that highlights descriptions of what he calls the affiliation, power, and achievement needs.[3] These are roughly parallel to Maslow's affiliation, esteem, and self-actualization needs.

Power introduces a category that is sometimes even harder for churches to deal with than status. McClelland sees it manifested in forcefulness, perseverance, and a leadership drive to influence others. In those terms, fellowship-building churches may need members with strong power motives even more than these people need to express their drive in churches. The achievement need expresses itself in the desire for unique accomplishments. It has interesting implications for viewing the exercise of spiritual gifts in churches. Effective leaders usually display a dominant personal coupling of achievement and power needs.

A model that will be perhaps most appealing to church leaders is offered by Clayton Alderfer. He simplifies Maslow's hierarchy into three categories:

existence needs (bodily and security)
relatedness needs (affiliation and esteem)
growth needs (development of human potential)

In his view the order in which they have to be satisfied before progressing on to the next is less significant. All needs can motivate at the same time.[4]

The difficulty of the task of identifying needs has led to another direction of theorizing that will be only mentioned here. This is to sidestep the question of motives and to concentrate on satisfactions. Focusing on reinforcement, this approach looks only at incentives that bring more of the desired behavior. If an offering of reward under certain conditions is associated with an increase in expected action, improved performance requires careful administration of such reinforcement. The most well-known advocate is B. F. Skinner with his theory of operant conditioning.

Because of this result-oriented practical thrust, such theorizing has gained increased acceptance among practitioner psy-

---

[3] David C. McClelland, *The Achieving Society* (Von Nostrand, 1967).

[4] Clayton Alderfer, *Existence, Relatedness, and Growth* (Free Press, 1972).

chologists and managers in recent years. Ministers are likely to have difficulty with the assumptions of this approach, but at the practical level they often wind up applying its advice: do more of what works.

Exploration Topic C: Looking for the Holy Spirit

Where does the Holy Spirit fit into the discussion of how to move Christians? Isn't the Spirit a prime mover? What is the relationship between understanding the work of the Spirit and insights from motivational psychology?

Scripture gives us two ways to recognize the Holy Spirit's moving presence among Christians: by the fruit He brings and the gifts He gives.

Paul describes the fruit of the Spirit in Gal. 5:22: "The fruit of the Spirit is love, joy, peace, patience, kindness, goodness, faithfulness, gentleness, and self-control." Central to all these is love. Spirit-induced love is the basis for all the virtues of Christian living.

How can this basic Christian motivation be related to the need-based psychology of the previous section? One possibility is to see the fruit of the Spirit as the way needs are expressed. Bodily, security, and affiliation needs may well remain as strong in a Christian as in a neighbor or working partner who is not a believer. But the Spirit guides the Christian in the search for the means of filling those needs. The Spirit at work leads the individual to reject many alternatives and to pursue others that demonstrate love to others at the same time that it satisfies the individual's need. What applies to believers applies to their church, too. Whatever leadership exists in a church, it is most faithful when it stimulates and demonstrates the virtuous fruit of the Spirit.

The other way to recognize the Holy Spirit is to look for his gifts. Paul teaches extensively about this part of the Spirit's work in Rom. 12, 1 Cor. 12, and Eph. 4. The Corinthian passage is the most developed:

> There are different kinds of gifts, but the same Spirit. There are different kinds of service, but the same Lord. There are different kinds of working, but the same God works all of them in all men. Now to each one the manifestation of the Spirit is

given for the common good. . . . All these (wisdom, knowledge, faith, miraculous powers, prophecy, discernment, speaking in tongues, and interpretation) are the work of one and the same Spirit, and He gives them to each one, just as He determines. (1 Cor. 12:4–11)

In Paul's usage, the gifts of the Spirit are something beyond the virtuous living that should be seen in all Christians. These are the special contributions a church member is moved to make for the common good. The lists of these gifts are different, with some overlap, in the three letters. A precise identification is not important. The point is that the Spirit will move each member of the body to do something special for the others.

In terms of motivational psychology, these gifts can be considered a special need that the Spirit instills in each. We might even think of it as the highest self-actualization need in the Maslow hierarchy. Doing something for the common good develops as an inner push. It then is there for the fellowship to pull into use.

If one assumes that each member has such a push, as Paul states, then the leadership challenge becomes apparent. Peter states it in 1 Peter 4:10: "Each one should use whatever gifts he has received to serve others, faithfully administering God's grace in its various forms." With such dynamics at work among fellowship members, there should be no lack of energy to engage and guide. The question is how well the members and leaders are looking for the fruits and gifts of the Holy Spirit. When they consciously know what they are looking for, the Spirit and his inner push are more likely to be found.

Chapter 5 _____

Building Fellowship Sharing

Consider these cases:

1. *The Potluck*

The Sunday-evening potluck at Chapel Grove Church was going well, as usual. About 120 were in attendance. The serving table was loaded with specialty dishes, and people were going back for seconds. Children were darting back and forth. Groups of adults were in conversation. The couples who had organized the event looked pleased. With people in good spirits, the evening advanced to a time of praise and prayer led by the pastor.

The hospitality committee at South Forks Church was discussing whether to try another Sunday-evening potluck. The church members were apparently too busy for this activity. Attendance was down, but the organizers were even more concerned that fewer dishes were showing up. They knew that they would have to provide more of the food themselves. But the funds collected last time were not enough, and they were getting tired of worrying and working so hard. Even the worship time seemed discouraging.

The potluck dinners at the church in Corinth were not going well at all. Some members were having a great time, but others felt humiliated and wondered why they had come. It had become not so much a shared meal as a bunch of private picnic lunches held in the same area. There was almost no sharing. Some groups turned their lunch into a feast and even got drunk. Others were left to watch and feel how hungry their few bites of food left them. Their time of worship and receiving the Lord's body and blood did little to draw them together; it just seemed to make them judge each other with more hostility (1 Cor. 11:17–33).

2. The Sunday School

The children's Sunday school at Grace Church was growing in size. It had about 80 children and 10 teachers. There was a feeling in the church that all were in this together. The parents found that their children usually looked forward to the Sunday school hour and consistently brought them. The teachers were usually well prepared, and they felt appreciated by the families and others in the church. There was actually a waiting list for new teachers.

The Sunday school superintendent at Trinity Church was debating whether to resign. She did not know what more she could do to get new teachers. Some barely stayed a few months, and now two long-time faithful teachers were leaving. They felt tired of giving so much and getting so little in return for the effort. The children were disrespectful—if they came at all. The parents did not seem to care, and the rest of the members hardly noticed the teachers. Everybody assumed that there should be a Sunday school, but hardly anyone wanted to do anything about it.

3. The Mission Church

Columbia Church started as a mission 10 years ago. The original core of members worked hard to reach others. Thankful for what the fellowship meant to them, the members took a big leap of faith in the third year to pool their financial resources and start a building program. With expanded membership they increased their budget commitment in the sixth year and added another staff member. In their tenth year they have an average of 250 worshipers, a full set of church programs, a staff of three, and a physical plant valued at $1,000,000 (carrying a mortgage of $700,000).

Calvary Church started as a mission 10 years ago. It is still a mission. The membership has been about the same for the last four years. They operate with a budget of $45,000, including the rent for a Sunday facility and

74

an office. Five years ago they came close to buying a church building that was being vacated, but they finally decided that they did not have enough financial commitments to assume such a large debt. The current pastor is their third. Over the years they have tried several programs, but cannot seem to make them last long. Some of the original members are talking about moving on to a more established church where they will not have to carry so much of the burden themselves.

4. *The Jerusalem Fellowship*

When the first Christian church in Jerusalem was a mission, it was made up of new believers whom the Holy Spirit moved mightily so that they "were together and had everything in common." They shared their meals together with good and sincere hearts. "Selling their possessions and goods," they pooled their resources and took care of those among them who had need. "No one claimed any of his possessions was his own, but they shared everything they had." The expectation that they share fully was so strong that some (Ananias and Sapphira) even lied to claim that they had given all they owned—with disastrous personal consequences.

In this fellowship the giving was accompanied by expectations of receiving in return. The Greek members complained strongly when their widows did not receive their appropriate share of the daily distribution of food made available by the combined resources. The sharing was then more carefully administered by Stephen and six colleagues (Acts 2:44–47; 4:32; 5:1–10; 6:1–4).

The Jerusalem mission, of course, grew; the Lord consistently added to their numbers. Certainly, the Spirit-led sharing that was basic to their life together was also basic to their effectiveness in reaching out and reaching upward in their ministry and mission.

Administration of the common meal, now the Eucharist, and of the shared offering remained necessary and over time became the special responsibility of the bishop, or overseer, who also took on broader responsibilities for maintaining and protecting the fellowship and its exchanges.

The common denominator in all these descriptions of church life is sharing—people giving to each other and receiving from each other.

In a potluck dinner, the sharing is obvious, and dinners in which many people receive without contributing soon are not repeated. Or as the Corinthians found, gatherings in which people give of their presence without receiving start falling apart.

Any church program involving a shared effort, such as a Sunday school, depends on members both giving of their time and energy and also receiving something of worth in return. When the sharing gets out of balance, as with teachers who feel that they receive little help or appreciation, programs deteriorate or even collapse.

Churches grow when participants find moving experiences of God's presence. But the members also have to give of their personal and financial resources so that the congregation can expand its services and reach out to more people. Churches in which the giving is minimal stay minimal.

The sharing in a Christian congregation can be breathtaking—as evidenced by the first Christians in Jerusalem, who sold everything so they could make available to the church all that they had. But even there, a proper balance between giving and receiving was necessary.

Sharing is a fundamental act of fellowship. The word *fellowship* means being in partnership with others in a joint undertaking. The Greek word is *koinōnia*, which basically means having something in common or sharing something with somebody.

Chapter 7 will expand this definition of fellowship beyond the act of sharing into a comprehensive description of the people who do the sharing—the community. Thus the word has two meanings, the broader referring to a group of believers who are committed to sharing their life in Christ with each other. The focus in this chapter is on the understanding of *fellowship* as the simple process of sharing, which is the basic building act of community.

Building Fellowship Exchanges

To build fellowship is to build sharing among participants. The task can be understood more clearly by distinguishing between leader efforts that help people receive from others and efforts that help people give to others. Such sharing can be seen

76

as exchanges between individuals and even between the larger group, or fellowship, and those who would participate in it. The basic fellowship exchange can be envisioned this way:

First Person's Resources	————>	Other Person's Needs
First Person's Needs	<————	Other Person's Resources

In the simple illustration of a potluck, the first person may offer a meat dish, which the second person needs as part of a full meal because she brought a vegetable dish, which the first person in turn needs as part of a full meal. In this back and forth flow of resources and needs sharing occurs, and this builds as more people join the flow and the participants find more needs that can be matched with resources.

The larger fellowship of gathered members builds as their combined resources are offered to meet needs of individuals, who contribute their personal resources to replenish or add to the fellowship's resources. This exchange can be envisioned as:

Church Resources	————>	Person's Needs
Church Needs	<————	Person's Resources

What are some examples of the sharing that this exchange represents?

Church Resources	————>	*Person's Needs*
The Gospel		Salvation
God's Word		Health
Sacraments		Security
Worship events		Affiliation
Nurturing activities		Esteem
Care and service		Growth
Relationships		

Church Needs	<————	*Person Resources*
Committed members		Renewed Life
Participation		Identification with church
Energy		Presence
Leadership		Love
Money		Gratitude
		Money

A church's resources are recognizable especially as the visible events that it offers in worship, education, care and service, and witnessing. The more serious a church is about making such efforts, the more likely it is to develop a formal program that will involve members and others in these events. A church's needs are basically to replenish and increase its resources of member energy, time, and funds so that it can repeat and extend its offerings in the future. Most churches rightfully envision themselves as sources of giving to others. But they cannot do so without also receiving the human means with which to make the offerings occur. The exchange process is basic to church life.

There are two phases in the exchange cycle in which attention can be most effectively focused in order to build the exchange. Or put negatively, insufficient attention to these two phases can result in a reduction of exchange and a deterioration of programs. The two points are:

1. Assuring that a church's offering will be received by individuals
2. Assuring that individuals recognize expectations for their giving

The first phase concerns the offering transaction in the exchange diagram:

Church Resources ————————> Person's Needs

Assuring that the resources are better offered to meet individual needs is the focus of the next section on "Helping Seekers Become Finders."

The second phase is the return transaction:

Church Needs <———————— Person's Resources

Assuring that a church receives the flow of individual resources is the focus of the following section on "Shaping Fellowship Role Expectations."

If the approach of this chapter with its emphasis on exchange and transactions strikes the reader as theologically questionable, read the next chapter, in which a necessary balance is restored.

A common reaction to this way of looking at church life is that Christians ought to give without expecting a return. But if one keeps in mind a broad understanding of what believers can and should return to Christ and His church, the model can be helpful in opening up new insights.

Jesus knew about giving and receiving. When He healed 10 lepers and only one came back to thank Him, He made it clear that He expected all 10 to come back and give praise to God (Luke 17:17). In Gethsemane He expected Peter, James, and John to give Him the loyalty of wakefulness in His time of sorrow (Mark 14:37). For those who wanted to participate in His death and resurrection, He wanted in return that they deny themselves, take up their cross, and follow him (Mark 8:34).

The apostle Paul understood exchange in church life. In his letter to the Romans he repeated a concern shared several times with the churches that he had founded. He wanted to collect an offering for the poor saints in Jerusalem, and this was his appeal: "If the Gentiles have shared in the Jews' spiritual blessing, they owe it to the Jews to share with them their material blessings" (Rom. 15:27). To the Philippians Paul expressed his thanks that they shared in his troubles at a time when no other church "shared with me in the matter of giving and receiving. . . . Not that I am looking for a gift, but I am looking for what may be credited to your account" (Phil. 4:15, 17).

The first church in Jerusalem remains the clearest example of mutual giving and receiving, as noted in the introduction to this chapter.

The Offering Transaction: The Gospel Meeting Needs

John Davidson came to church several weeks ago with a friend. He felt good about the experience and was back the next Sunday.

Sarah Adams dropped her children off for Sunday school but did not stay for adult Bible class. She had attended several times a year ago and decided this was not for her.

Ellen Smith was at the desk in the church office bright and early on Thursday. This was her day to help as a volunteer. She looked forward to Thursdays.

Bill Brecht came to the young adults gathering Sunday evening. It seemed pretty flat and he did not feel that he got to know anybody. As he left, he thought he might try again next week, but he wasn't sure.

Each of these people came into contact with a program offered by a church. Consider what happened in terms of this image:

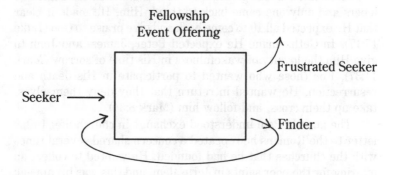

The box represents a specific offering of a congregation, best pictured as an event, happening, interaction, gathering, or activity at a specific time in the life of a congregation, such as a Sunday morning worship service, a particular Bible class session, a specific Thursday morning volunteer work day, a Tuesday callers evening, or a Saturday morning community service effort. Use "event" as the overall term for these occasions. Picture each event as happening within the same week—perhaps the third week in February. There may be dozens of events that week, most of which are part of some program, although not necessarily. A church will have all sorts of beliefs, goals, plans, and values, but until they "happen" in an event, they have not really become an offering.

The Seekers are people who come to participate in these events. Each participant is a seeker each time. Some may be first-time seekers; most will be repeaters. What each seeks will be slightly different, not only from person to person but from event to event. What is sought will be determined largely by their needs at that time. One approach to recognizing those needs was presented in chapter 4 under "Exploratory Topic B: Motivational Psychology."

The Finders are people whose needs were met. What happened addressed what they were looking for. Ideally, the Holy Spirit found them through the Gospel offered in the event so that faith was nurtured and spiritual needs satisfied. If given another opportunity, most will return to have the same or other needs met. They will return as Seekers at a later event. John Davidson and Ellen Smith are Finders.

The Frustrated Seekers are those whose needs were not met. The event did not address enough of their needs to leave them feeling satisfied with the experience. Some may try the event again later, but several frustrating experiences will probably take them out of the loop for that kind of event in the future. Sarah Adams and Bill Brecht are frustrated seekers.

Overall, the vitality and size of a congregation will depend on Seekers becoming Finders or, more specifically, on the proportion of Seekers who become Finders. Fellowship exchange and a community life of fellowship are hard to maintain when many of the Seekers are frustrated in their search, when the Holy Spirit is limited by a limited sharing of the Gospel. Fellowship life will be lively and grow when the Gospel has free course and most previous and new Seekers become Finders *over and over again.*

This image and the definitions of Seeker—event offering—finder are important to the extent that they guide thinking about how to improve the way in which the Gospel-based transactions of the fellowship offering flow to and are accepted by various persons. The giving and receiving of fellowship starts with the offering from the already shared resources of the fellowship. It will not go far if the offering is received by only a few people. Almost worse is to have the Offering Event tried by many Seekers of whom only a few become repeat Finders.

As should be apparent in the way the issue is framed, the key to improving transactions is the design of each event offering. Will it help Seekers become Finders? How can the event more effectively turn Seekers into Finders?

Engineering and Marketing Approaches

There are two basic approaches to designing what a church will offer to build fellowship sharing. One is to start with what those arranging the event consider important. The other is to start with recognizing and responding to what potential participants are seeking.

Typically, church leaders are more comfortable offering what they are familiar with and know how to do. This is especially so with pastors, whose special study and experience keep them close to the rich resources of Scriptural understandings and centuries of church practices. The Christian church has so much to offer. In deciding what to emphasize, program planners may project onto others what they find important for themselves—what has turned their seeking into a finding. Often they make good matches and others respond. From this perspective, these program leaders are like engineers designing what seems best to them. Based on their training and experience, engineers determine what should be done and how to do it.

Worship services and Bible studies often have this engineering flavor. A pastor may use a liturgical form that has been commonly practiced in previous generations, assuring the participants that they will learn to like what has stood the test of time. Or the Bible study may be primarily a lecture presentation of exegetical insights into a portion of Scripture, leaving each participant to make his or her own application.

The other approach is to recognize what needs will be addressed before determining the offering. Will those who come be seeking primarily new knowledge, practical insights for daily living, inspirational experiences, a time of friendly togetherness, or something else? How many potential participants are there for each of these emphases? What events have helped them become finders before?

From this perspective, program planners are more like marketers who focus on the "market" and concentrate not on their own needs and experiences but on the needs and experiences of those they are trying to reach. From that understanding, they can work at shaping an offering to meet what those who are to be "pulled" into the event are looking for.

Marketers cannot replace engineers. This is true in business, where the product offered must perform as promised, reliably and safely. This is especially true in churches, where fellowship offerings must remain faithful to God's Word. But marketers can point out what engineers should focus on. Pastors themselves can become more comfortable wearing two hats: the necessary theological engineer's hat but also the helpful administrative marketer's hat. And they can become more comfortable with putting on the marketer's hat first when trying to develop a program.

Further development of marketing insights for church leaders is presented in this chapter as "Exploration Topic A: A Marketing Approach to Managing Exchanges." It draws on the work of Philip Kotler, a leading professor of marketing for nonprofit organizations.

The Return Transaction: Shaping Fellowship Role Expectations

Helping Seekers become Finders addresses the first transaction of the fellowship exchange. The second, the return transaction, concerns the flow of a person's resources back to meeting the church's need for replenishing and expanding its resources. It challenges the church to take steps to assure that this phase of fellowship exchange happens well enough for a church to have more to offer in initiating future exchanges.

The image of *role* can be helpful to highlight where to focus leadership energy for this effort. The analogy is drawn from the theater, where certain people act out words and motions determined for them by a playwright and a director. The actors in a play perform according to what somebody else expects of them. They take an assigned role for the sake of sharing in the presentation of a story.

Social psychologists have expanded the concept of *role* to include any set of behavior patterns expected of a person in relation to others. These occur in families, for instance, with the roles of mother, father, or oldest child. From this perspective, organizations are full of highly differentiated and fairly well-defined roles like secretary, supervisor, treasurer, or president. For the sake of shared endeavor, participants let the expectations of others determine much of what they do. As their relationships multiply, they may take on several different roles in their various interactions.

The concept is helpful for a better understanding of why individuals in shared endeavor behave the way they do and how their behavior might be better adapted to desired outcomes. What expectations are they responding to, and where did these come from? In any situation, what role are they performing, and what do they think belongs or does not belong to that role? A cooperative endeavor can be improved by changing and refining the role messages that participants recognize and that influence their behavior. To some extent, performance disappointments or conflict can be reduced by better definition and communication of role expectations. This amounts to doing a better job of telling participants what is expected of them.

In applying this analogy to churches, one can ask, What role expectations for fellowship sharing exist now within a congregation? If there is disappointment with the level of actual fellowship exchange, how much of this can be attributed to low expectations for such sharing to occur? What kind of fellowship performance is defined and encouraged by current role expectations?

Christians may not be accustomed to talking about role performance within the church, although people occasionally discuss such issues as the role of a Christian in dealing with a social issue such as caring for the homeless or facing the arms race. But within a congregation, members expect many things of each other, however scattered and inconsistent their expectations may be. In a worship service itself, participants let their behavior be influenced by others as they stand, sing, or pray when people around them do. How far beyond the worship role does a member let church role expectations extend?

Fellowship *performance* is an appropriate concern for Christian churches. Fellowship itself is not just a verbal ideal or symbol. It is the sustained activity of sharing something in common, the mutual interaction of people who belong to the same community, the reciprocal giving and receiving of what one person has and a fellow member needs. As noted, the Greek word for "fellowship" is *koinōnia*, from the root word for "common," with the added dimension of participation in whatever that common thing is. Based on its theological underpinnings of sharing the same God in Christ, Christian koinonia is essentially a community action or performance concept.

Role performance of *shallow fellowship* can be seen in churches where there is hardly any interaction of members at all beyond Sunday morning—and maybe not much even then. For whatever reasons, the members have learned to expect little of each other, and they have become accustomed to giving little of themselves in response. They perform only limited church roles. Fellowship builders will want to know how the prevalent role developed. They may discover that over the years such limited performance is all that was expected and modeled. Even when they do talk about fellowship, churches get what they deserve when they understand it to mean nothing more than chatting over

84

coffee and cookies during a social time after the worship hour or the hall where "fellowship events" are supposed to happen. Role performance of *lively fellowship*, by God's grace, can be found where members interact frequently, perhaps several times a week, in diverse shared activities of their Christian response or when they can often be seen extending a service to others as well as willingly receiving help from them. In a church characterized by lively fellowship performance, most members expect much of each other and give of themselves accordingly. "Togetherness" includes prayer, Bible study, and mission outreach efforts, as well as socials and entertaining times. Lively fellowship performance happens when members act within the broad, well-developed church roles. Not coincidentally, the lively building stones usually outnumber the passive ones. Building lively fellowship performance becomes the purpose for a fellowship building ministry. Working with role expectations is one of the basic tools for doing so. Raising expectations and thereby performance is a leadership challenge that calls for faithful vision, clear definition by planning and organizing, and deliberate formation of allegiance, as discussed in subsequent chapters. There is more on shaping role expectations in this chapter's "Exploration Topic B: Send Convincing Role Messages."

Exploration Topic A:
A Marketing Approach to Better Exchanges

Why bother fitting church life into the somewhat alien concept of "exchange"? Because that framework provides considerable help in figuring out how to build sharing relationships. Church leaders can profit from the accumulated management experience of how to talk about, plan, and administer exchanges. The discipline that does this the most directly is *marketing*. Although at first glance it may appear that there is little relation between secular marketing and church program development, much is to be found there. The concepts are relevant, even though the usual business applications may not be. Philip Kotler develops the fundamental theme of exchange in *Marketing for Non-Profit Organizations*.[1]

The central question for church leaders is, How can sharing

---

[1] Philip Kotler, *Marketing for Non-profit Organizations* (1st ed.; Prentice Hall, 1975).

relationships within a fellowship be improved? Of course, improvement begins with hearing God's call anew and depends on the operation of the Holy Spirit. Yet from the human perspective, churches do some things that aid interaction and some things that become barriers. Marketers would say that insights for better management of exchanges can come from assessing the four Ps: Product, Place, Promotion, and Price. Each is clearly relevant to church program development and leadership.

The most important element to understand is *product*. This means the offering extended to another. If the offering is something the person is seeking, exchange will probably happen, so long as the offering is appropriately available and the person knows about it. If it is not something for which there is a seeker, there will be no returning finders, regardless of how it is offered. While *product* would be a jarring term to describe a Sunday morning worship service, the concept has potential to open up many insights about the varying needs that a specific event can touch.

Place means the location where an offering is made available. Whether to foster Bible study in the church building or in participants' homes is a regular planning question, and in recent years there has been a strong trend toward locating this activity in members' homes. Television presents a relatively new place for distributing Gospel offerings, but it is a context that does little to build fellowship.

Promotion is what most people think of when they hear about marketing. Promotion certainly has to be done, but it is probably the least important barrier to exchange. When the offering, distribution, and price are right, the event will happen with almost no promotion. When the other elements do not fit what people are looking for, the promotion will make little difference.

Price represents a barrier to what a person can receive and also a barrier to what the fellowship receives in return. Low-price and high-price strategies will need to be discussed.

Program Development as Product Development

As suggested, program development in churches corresponds roughly to product development in a business. Planning programs rationally is what the formal church organization does.

Much of church life is not cared for by the organization, but when the organization does purposely program an event within the fellowship, it is subject to many of the same dynamics with which other rational organizations must reckon in making a product offering.

As presented earlier in this chapter, there are two approaches to designing a product or an event offering. One is from the perspective of the person or group that wants to initiate the exchange. The other is from the perspective of the person or group that is to receive it. The easiest starting point is what the initiators know and can do. They project onto others what is important to themselves. Often they make a good match. From this perspective the program planners are like engineers designing what seems best to them. They see themselves knowing and offering what is significant.

Marketers start from the perspective of the intended recipients and what they are seeking. Marketers try to identify the needs that would motivate someone into the action of receiving the intended offering. Marketers see themselves as delivering satisfactions. They try to turn seekers into finders. Engineers must be involved in any substantial offering to assure its reliability and effectiveness.

In churches, theologians and keepers of tradition represent ecclesiastical engineers. If there could only be one perspective, the engineer's is the more important. Some have an intuitive feel for what people are seeking and how to address that need. But most could use the help that comes from rational application of marketing perspectives. This can assure greater effectiveness in building sharing relationships that become a full-bodied fellowship.

How would marketers arrive at insights for better design of the offering? Philip Kotler distinguishes three forms of offering that should be explored. The first is the *tangible product*—the one that is most apparent in a generic sense. In businesses this might be a vehicle with four wheels and an engine, or an ointment used to color lips.

The second is the *core product*—the basic benefit or need satisfaction that is offered. Some core needs are security, health, or affiliation (see chapter 4). Core needs might be the hope of beauty that a woman brings to the selection of a lipstick or the sense of status that can go into buying a car. A merchant is not just selling shoes (the tangible offering) but is offering a benefit, such as fashion or comfort.

A third approach to the offering is what Kotler calls the *augmented product* or package. This is how the offering appears when it is finally packaged and the potential recipient makes a decision about it. "Packaging" is usually the marketing term with which church leaders are least uncomfortable. Many decisions go into program development, and changing any one of them means changing the package. Determining the augmented product— packaging it—is done most purposefully and rationally by first determining the core need to be addressed.

How many different ways can the Gospel be packaged faithfully and effectively? More than most church leaders realize.

To pick a couple of examples, recall the needs highlighted by Maslow. Can the Gospel appeal to bodily needs? In His ministry, Jesus certainly sought to heal the sick and the lame in view of spiritual healing and wholeness. Some churches today package the Gospel in ministries led by deaconesses, parish nurses, social workers, and counselors.

Christian churches have been exceptionally effective at ministering to the security needs of people. These might include a sense of predictability about life and protection from harm. Scripture certainly speaks to such a need with messages of God's control over life and such images as a rock and a fortress. For many churchgoers the familiar routine of a worship service addresses the core need for secure predictability, and worship packaging that departs from the familiar will bring strong resistance.

Affiliation seems to be a strong need in current American society, and many churches have learned to package their Gospel offerings around small-group interaction.

Esteem can be addressed somewhat through a worship service packaged with exceptional music and fine vestments for the leader.

These examples are intended only as suggestions that might trigger other associations of church offerings with human core needs. Starting with those needs is characteristic of a marketer.

Pricing Strategy

Pricing is another business term that seems out of place in church life. But again it is the concept that is important. Pricing refers to what the initiators of an exchange expect in return. In churches money is only one of many possible returns. Why does an offering need a return? To replenish the resources of the initiator. The merchant must expect the means to replenish stock. If a store gives everything away, it would soon be out of business and a help to no one. That businesses also look for a profit beyond their costs does not necessarily prevent applying the analogy to churches that simply look for the means to replenish their resources.

What does price look like in a church? It consists of the things a church must have to be a lively fellowship. At a minimum a church expects a degree of thankfulness among recipients of a service offered. Members are not likely to continue the community service if they are ignored or abused in the process. Among people who are edging into the fellowship life, price might consist simply of their time and presence at future events. They cannot receive if they are not there. For people who are drawing closer into fellowship life, the expectations might include the recipients' return of their energy and skills in reaching out to others. Most fellowships might expect participants to agree with the beliefs central to their shared identity before God. Some might also expect participants to behave differently. Financial contributions are usually included in the expected responses, but presumably as part of a range of responses that include time, energy, and talent to provide resources for future events in the fellowship. In short, the price of being in a fellowship is that individuals join in the sharing interactions that are basic to fellowship.

Looking at response in terms of price allows the overall building strategy of a congregation to be recognized as either a low-price or a high-price approach. A low-price strategy sets minimal expectations for presence, identity, beliefs, changed behavior, and the sharing of energy and dollars. There is clear rationale for this approach in daily life. The lower the price of goods or services, the more takers there will be.

One does not have to look far to recognize churches that either purposefully or unconsciously settle into a low-price strategy for their offering. They talk little about distinctive beliefs for fear of offending someone. There is no perceptual difference in their behavior in comparison to the society around them. Little is said about attendance, and in general, participants find that few expectations are held out for them.

How effective is such a strategy for building fellowship? It is hard to imagine how a lively, full-bodied fellowship could emerge under these circumstances. Such a church eventually has little to offer because it has asked for so little in return. Low expectations yield low sharing. Because sharing is minimal, expectations must be minimal in order to continue.

A church with a high-price strategy is not reluctant to set high expectations for participants. The more they share themselves and their time and energy, the more the fellowship has to offer. Dean Kelly's study titled *Why Conservative Churches Are Growing*[2] finds a strong correlation between growing denominations and denominations whose churches are demanding of their members. The demand can focus on beliefs (inerrant Bible), behavior (no alcoholic drink), financial contributions (a tithe or even a triple tithe), or readiness to witness to their faith.

But for a church simply to demand more of its people would not in itself build a fuller fellowship. The push into action must come from a response to God's call and from the movement of His Holy Spirit. A full-bodied Christian fellowship must be built around the members' fellowship with Christ and the Holy Spirit. With that core in place, expectations for sharing would yield a wide-ranging fellowship life among various churches.

Exploration Topic B: Sending Convincing Role Messages

How can role expectations be better shaped so that they elicit the desired performance? Generally, by sending out a greater variety of clearer, more convincing role messages.

Participants learn expectations for their behavior from many sources—what they carry in their own memories, are told by a leader, see others doing, are told by their friends, or read in formal statements of expectations. For present purposes, the more that these sources communicate lively fellowship performance expectations, the greater is the probability that participants' expectations will be shaped in that direction. The church leadership challenge is to be aware of which, if any, fellowship-related messages are currently being communicated through all available channels and then purposefully to develop these mes-

---

[2] Dean Kelly, *Why Conservative Churches Are Growing* (Harper and Row, 1977).

sages so that they are more supportive of the Christ-centered fellowship-building endeavor.

Deliberately presenting a variety of message sources is important because people differ in their ability to receive and learn from communication. A combination that works well for one person may have little impact on another. Some hear and translate abstract concepts readily. Others have to be shown before they derive meaning. Some rely on friends to filter and interpret what is important. Others respond to written definitions of how and with whom they should interact. The more varied the sources and the more complete the messages from them, the greater is the likelihood that a wide variety of church members will attach significance to what is being communicated—and act accordingly.

One-way verbal messages, from the speaker to a hearer without a chance for response, are the easiest to deliver and are readily offered in churches. Yet research consistently shows that hearers typically receive only a small proportion of the words, which typically have little influence. Fellowship builders will want to determine what role expectations are actually being projected in these frequent messages. But lively fellowship seldom develops from this source alone.

Action messages are the most pervasive in a fellowship, either by their presence or absence. People learn by doing. Members are surrounded by what they see others doing or not doing and this influences their own behavior. Technique (or technology) means the accepted way of doing something. A church's techniques for worship or Bible study, for instance, will convey messages about whether members are expected to act on their own or in shared interaction with others. Are a church's current action techniques contributing to fellowship building or detracting from it?

Informal group messages are the most powerful sources that affect people. So say the social psychologists. When confronting conflicting messages, an individual will respond to the one that comes mediated through the group to which he or she feels the most attraction. People relate more readily to 10 others than to 100. Does a church have a variety of groupings that appeal to different interests? What messages are they sending? Experienced fellowship builders know that stimulating the growth of supportive small groups is basic to developing a lively fellowship.

Formal agreements are the lasting promises that a person

91

makes and of which he or she can be reminded. Presented, for example, as constitutions, job descriptions, or pledges, such agreements are the framework of formal organizations. This can be one of the most convenient message sources with which to work. What messages about fellowship life does a church's formal structure send? What does it recognize as important enough to seek agreement from the members? Fellowship builders will want to assure themselves that the messages a church's organization sends out cover more than the members' role in relation to money and conflict.[3]

These categories of the sources of role messages are not just arbitrarily selected. They are adaptations of categories fundamental to the study of organizational behavior. In *The Restless Organization*, J. W. Hunt recognizes the focal importance of role in determining what people do in the course of a day or a year in a work organization. Then he asks what determines the expectations in the role system that constitutes an organization? What variables influence work behavior? He highlights four and makes these the outline for understanding organizational behavior. They are the individual's own personality, the technical system, the informal system, and the formal structure. These are the variables with which to work to improve organizational behavior.[4] In various forms, they are the common outline of most textbooks on the subject.

---

[3] Applications of these message sources to church life are developed more extensively in chapter 7 of *Pastoral Administration* by David Luecke and Samuel Southard (Word Publishing, 1986).

[4] John W. Hunt, *The Restless Organization* (John Wiley and Sons, 1972).

Chapter 6 _____

Building Fellowship Allegiance

The previous chapter on building fellowship exchanges may leave some readers unsettled. There must be more to church leadership than managing exchanges, satisfying seekers, and setting role expectations.

Indeed there is, but in the general area of leadership studies, knowing how to put a finger on it has been difficult. Finally, in recent years a vocabulary is becoming popular that distinguishes two types of leadership in a way that will be of interest especially to pastors. In a much-quoted work, James MacGregor Burns suggests that we consider *transactional leadership* and *transformational leadership*.[1]

Transactional leadership is what one most commonly sees, especially in organizations. Such leaders concentrate on developing exchanges among followers, recognizing what they want from their participation and how to respond to it. The followers' level of effort depends on their confidence that such effort will yield outcomes that they desire. Much of the practice and literature of management takes this approach. The previous chapter was essentially a discussion of transactional leadership applied to fellowship building.

Transformational leaders recognize and respond to existing needs of followers, but they go farther and seek to arouse and satisfy higher-level needs, to engage the person of the follower more fully. Transformation, in this sense, can be achieved by raising the followers' awareness or consciousness of the importance of designated outcomes and ways of reaching them. It means getting followers to transcend their own self-interest for the sake of the team, the organization, or the larger group. Such leadership brings performance beyond the initial expectations of

---

[1] James MacGregor Burns, *Leadership* (Harper and Row, 1978).

the followers.[2] In political life, examples of such transformational leaders are Roosevelt and Churchill, who both had a profound impact on their nations and brought forth widespread levels of performance that few would have anticipated.

Church leadership must seek to elevate members' consciousness of God's purposes, presence, and power and to help them grow beyond their self-interests to gain a greater commitment to God and His church as the body of Christ. Whatever else it is, church leadership must be transformational in nature. How much such leadership must be transactional as well is a continuing question. Seldom can a leader be effective at transformation without also paying attention to the transactions. Leadership is more than transaction, but it is seldom less than that. Thus the previous chapter's emphasis on exchange was necessary. But it is not sufficient.

Transactional leadership can account for simple program successes and exchanges. But it does not adequately explain how fellowship members go on to transcend everyday personal concerns and to be built together with firm membership commitments—how a church receives the loyalty of its members even when the visible exchanges become unbalanced, especially in adversity.

Transformational leadership—transforming people and transforming their allegiances—must occur in order for sturdy, long-lasting fellowship to be built. This chapter will present transformational leadership in the church as the challenge to build firm fellowship allegiance. Fundamentally, this is work for the Holy Spirit, as conveyed in the spiritual core of church life. It is also a task that can be advanced by the basic program processes of bringing members into frequent contact with each other under circumstances in which the Spirit can do His work.

Ligaments and Allegiance

In his usual way, the apostle Paul offers an image with much potential to open up new insights for providing transformational leadership. His body-of-Christ analogy highlights how the body is joined and held together by *ligaments*. We can picture these ligaments on an anatomy chart that shows how muscles and other

---

[2] Bernard W. Bass, *Leadership and Performance Beyond Expectations* (Free Press, 1985).

tissues are held together and fastened to the bones. Paul uses the image twice in a fellowship-building context.

From him the whole body, joined and held together by every supporting ligament, grows and builds itself up in love, as each part does its work. (Eph. 4:16)

[A boastful leader] has lost connection with the Head, from whom the whole body, supported and held together by its ligaments and sinews, grows as God causes it to grow. (Col. 2:19)

When the ligaments are in place and strong, the result is *allegiance*, a word that comes from the same Latin root as ligament. Allegiance to one's church is like the allegiance a person pledges to his or her country. It emphasizes the needs of the larger entity, be it country or church.

To build strong allegiance in a church is to bind members tightly together. Poorly developed, skimpy ligaments produce a church with weak allegiance. Such a church would be dominated by members who do not stay associated much beyond the point where their immediate needs are satisfied. Weak allegiance is evident when believers move from one congregation to another, receiving more from the fellowship than they give. Strong allegiance is found among members who persist, even when they are not personally rewarded, and who generally give more than they receive in the fellowship exchange.

We will want to ask more carefully what ligaments look like in the church. What is it that joins, holds together, and supports the parts of Christ's body, the members of a church fellowship? Of course, the next question will be how church leaders can "build" more and firmer ligaments throughout the body.

But first let us note some other images for what allegiance represents. They have implications for leadership focus and activity.

A popular image is *involvement*, which conveys a sense of bringing people closer in. Church leaders often talk about ways to get a particular person more involved in the church, usually by finding a job or committee assignment for that person. This view and expression can be found in many secular clubs and groups. In itself, the image presents little of theological significance.

Better is *assimilation*, an image that has recently become more common among church leaders. It is a good summary term

95

for what Paul commends to the Philippians: "Make my joy complete by being like-minded, having the same love, being one in spirit and purpose" (Phil. 2:2). To be like-minded and have the same love is to be brought into similarity—to be assimilated. Assimilating new members is a necessary function that is usually done better when it is done deliberately. Assimilation, however, does not mean conformity to others in all aspects of church life, something that is neither possible nor particularly desirable.

Beyond involvement or assimilation, the best image for the process of building allegiance is *incorporation*. It means "to be formed into one body" and is thus a fitting description of what happens when the various parts of the body of Christ, the church, are brought together as one (1 Cor. 12:12–13) and held together with ligaments. Incorporation assumes a much higher degree of mutual commitment than does involvement or assimilation. One cannot be incorporated into the body of Christ without God's action.

Before looking at ways to build allegiance—to incorporate— we should recognize one other related image that can be helpful. Allegiance can be described as the *glue* that holds a church together, that makes the members *cohesive*. Lyle Schaller develops this image by discussing 20 possible glues in a congregation; undoubtedly more could be added. Some are stronger cohesive forces for incorporation than others. Some have little to do with building allegiance in a fellowship.

Schaller identifies these glues as likely to displace the focus of allegiance in congregations from fellowship in Christ to something else: kinfolk ties, social class, a building, denominational identity, the personality of the minister, the church secretary, the choir director, organizational structure, or liturgy. He maintains that the two best glues are the group life within a congregation and the program for ministry. He also commends a distinctive congregational lifestyle that appears in some churches and is described as participatory, celebrative, and relational.[3]

Schaller's observations can provide a sense of relief but also a necessary caution to church leaders. Allegiances are not always hard to form, and they can occur around a variety of common focuses in group life. But to build fellowship that truly belongs in the body of Christ means that church allegiances must develop

---

[3] Lyle E. Schaller, *Assimilating New Members* (Abingdon, 1978), 21–37.

for the right reason. The theme of allegiance is more extensively developed by Lawrence O. Richards and Clyde Hoeldtke in *A Theology of Church Leadership.*[4] The present discussion was stimulated by their work. They put the focus of members' allegiance to one another in the context of allegiance to the Father, the Son, and the Holy Spirit.

Providing for the Ligaments of Fellowship

What are the ligaments binding the members of the body of Christ together? How can they be strengthened?

When Paul uses this image, he does not define it. Here is an attempt: Think of fellowship ligaments as *fellowship interactions under the power of the Holy Spirit.* There are two components to his understanding—the interaction of members in fellowship and the movement of the Holy Spirit. Both need to be present to build a firm ligament. The first can be the special emphasis of transactional leadership. The second is transformational.

The range of possible fellowship interactions is practically unlimited. It can be as simple as two members talking with each other, perhaps informally over the telephone or on a planned basis in a home visit. It can be a group of church teenagers out for an evening or a youth Bible study. It can be 150 worshipers together on Sunday morning or a couples retreat. In all these cases, believers are interacting with other believers in the context of their mutual participation in a church fellowship.

The emphasis on believers in visible contact with other believers is necessary if the focus is to be on building the fellowship in a local congregation, especially if such overall fellowship becomes the defining characteristic of the congregation, as will be developed more fully in the next chapter. This is different from fellowship in a mostly symbolic sense. Under the power of the Holy Spirit a believer can be considered a part of the body of Christ and yet have little interaction with other believers. It can also be correct to think of the church in the abstract sense of all believers worldwide over all time, but that level of generalization involves a vastly different notion of fellowship, one that is quite hard to build on a day-by-day basis.

In concrete, lively local church fellowship, members cannot

---

[4] Lawrence O. Richards and Clyde Hoeldtke, *A Theology of Church Leadership* (Zondervan, 1980).

97

be joined together without being in contact with each other. A construction illustration shows the importance of frequent contact for making strong joints. One of the greatest challenges in woodworking is to join two pieces of wood together in a way that is strong and graceful. Nailing and screwing might do in rough work, but for finished work the best approach is to glue the parts together. The strength of such a joint depends on how much the surfaces of the two pieces are held in contact with each other by the glue. A molded, shaped configuration that, with its various wiggles, produces two inches of glued surface will be stronger than one with only one straight inch of surface. Look at the joints of a wooden window frame, for example. Fellowship interaction can be like a straight line with the minimum contact between members. Or it can have wiggles of additional interactions during the week or for extra purposes. A fellowship with the latter is more likely to have firmer ligaments. How to develop more interactions was the subject of the previous chapter.

But there must be more than contact to bring strong allegiance. Those in contact must have a purpose that transcends their personal needs. This is why the most frequent use of *allegiance* refers to loyalty to one's country. Where loyalty is high, citizens are ready to give higher priority to the country's needs than to their own, even to the point of self-sacrificial death. Leadership that produces such allegiance can effectively move people beyond their own self-interest to higher values and commitments.

Secular leaders have only their wits and persuasive power to fashion allegiance. Church leaders are not so limited to achieve transformational leadership. They have the Holy Spirit. There can be a significant difference in the result.

Episcopalian professor James W. Jones studied various voluntary communities, especially those that arose in the 1960s. He found that few survived for long, and that is true also of many other community efforts over the centuries. The ones that did survive were religious.

His explanation is that the others did not share enough beyond their direct relationship to stay cohesive under the pressures that inevitably occur in life together. James Jones notes, "From the standpoint of the Gospel, community remains a clear imperative. Only conversion, not ideology or theology or therapy, can create the self-transcendence that creates community. The

98

secular world will never produce abiding koinonia for it cannot get out of itself."[5]

Jones is affirming that community cannot be created by human effort. It is not a natural human possibility. Koinonia is a gift of the Spirit. It is an experience, a style of living. Organizational leadership plays a part, but only in a limited way:

> Structure and organization are important but they are derived. They do not create community, they only express koinonia if it is present. They must grow naturally out of the more basic experience of a community. Concentrating on organization as a means to community will construct only a skeleton, not a living body.[6]

The process itself of interacting with others brings some changes to people. But the power of the Holy Spirit brings greater and more lasting changes. Fellowship interactions are important as the occasions in which the Holy Spirit is present through Word-and-Sacrament ministries. The God-given gift of His presence and power produces the most significant changes in His followers and thereby changes their interaction.

To be better fellowship builders, church leaders need competence in conveying the means of spiritual transformation. In doctrinal terms these are the means of grace, the Word and sacraments. In spiritual leadership the constant challenge is to hear God speaking through His Word and with well-honed skills to apply that Word to the life of individuals and the whole fellowship, opening avenues for the Holy Spirit to have special impact on people.

The Christian church has a tremendous wealth of accumulated leadership experience in hearing and applying God's Word to transform people, experience gathered worldwide over the centuries. Preaching is the central, most visible activity, supplemented with various forms of teaching. Underlying these applications are exegetical skills for studying Scripture. A method for extending this teaching function that is regaining emphasis is the mutual sharing of God's Word by church members gathered in small-group settings. Here the Gospel message can be verbalized in everyday language and related to everyday concerns, as well

---

[5] James W. Jones, *The Spirit and the World* (Hawthorne, 1975), p. 42.

[6] Ibid., p. 43.

as demonstrated in action. Such informal speaking and hearing of God's Word as "mutual conversation and consolation of brethren" was recognized by Martin Luther as a means of grace (Smalcald Articles, Part III, Article IV).

The Word certainly has power that exceeds the frailties of its human presenters. But in the long experience of the Christian church it is apparent that attempts at transformational leadership have limited impact unless the leaders themselves are personally transformed by the Spirit to an exemplary level of Christ-centered faith, love, and commitment. This lesson has been somewhat neglected in the emphasis on clergy professionalism seen in some quarters of pastoral development in the past several generations. A renewed emphasis on personal growth in the Spirit and on spiritual disciplines among pastors and church leaders is an increasingly evident corrective.

Exploration Topic A: A Political Approach to Building Church Allegiance

The previous discussion has emphasized two different approaches to building allegiance. One is the development of programs to increase interaction and exchanges within the fellowship, which is primarily administrative work. The other is the presentation of the means for spiritual transformation through speaking and hearing the Word of God, which is the thrust of preaching and teaching leadership.

Another necessary part of church life is sometimes approached as a means of allegiance building. This is the political approach toward the decision-making process, in which the fellowship arranges its internal affairs, establishes priorities, and distributes its resources. Almost by nature, this approach is controversial and is usually treated with caution by pastors. Although some leaders are inclined to regard it as a stimulator of allegiance, this approach is better seen as a way of expressing and shaping allegiance developed through the first two approaches.

"Politics" is a bad word for many church members and pastors, as it is for many participants in organized enterprises of all sorts—colleges, hospitals, the military, individual corporations. Some of that feeling may carry over from dissatisfaction with the most visible and unavoidable arena of politics, the political process of city, state, or national government. Much of it reflects disappointment that seemingly more rational and comprehensive decision making is not more common in matters affecting large numbers of participants. Faced with a decision they do not like or cannot understand, people are inclined to dismiss it as "just politics."

Suspicion of undisguised political activity arises from a different concern in churches. It reflects the belief that committed Christians are to be transformed by the Gospel and to be likeminded, which may involve an expectation that there will be no differences and thus no need for one group to try to exert power over another. According to this attitude, politics should be unnecessary, since it is about the accumulation and use of social or organizational power to achieve ends of special interest to one or another group within the larger entity. Reliance on such human mechanisms to exert dominance may seem unfaithful among God's people, besides appearing unseemly.

A wise and experienced university president once taught a junior administrator (the writer) a valuable perspective on organizational politics. The junior was much frustrated with an audacious and unexpected play for dominance from an influential trustee. Chancellor William H. Danforth of Washington University in St. Louis pointed to the plus in the situation—that the trustee at least cared about what the organization was doing and cared deeply enough to try to shape it. The opposite would be apathy or lack of passion. The university was better off with many involved leaders who cared deeply about its future than with having to rely on only a few leaders who faced widespread reluctance from others. The lesson learned was first to appreciate the riches of many different passions brought into organized effort and then to get on with finding ways to deal with them constructively.

Rather than dealing with apathy, churches are much better off with members who care deeply about the future of their fellowship. When they do, participants will work hard to see that their hopes are provided for, and the political process of exerting power is underway. The challenge for church leaders is to shape that process so the overall health and welfare of the fellowship is advanced.

Using a political approach to leadership is especially challenging in churches because of its presumption of diversity among

101

participants. The easier assumption and belief is that through their call by Christ into fellowship, believers are already of like mind and will agree on future actions without going through all the various maneuvers of gaining dominance, with their attendant pains and disruptions, that can be seen in other organizations.

Naive is one way to describe that assumption, as will be attested by legions of veteran pastors and denominational executives. It is also theologically superficial. According to the apostle Paul, diversity among fellowship participants does not represent a shortcoming in a church. It is a blessing. He writes to the Corinthians that differences in gifts, services, and workings are God-given through the Holy Spirit (1 Cor. 12:4–6). We can add that where there is diversity among participants, there will be different views of what is important and how to get at it. For leading amidst such blessings, political processes are inevitable, even in churches.

Rather than a starting point, Paul's charge to be "likeminded, having the same love, being one in spirit and purpose" (Phil. 2:2) is the intended outcome. This is the goal for efforts to build allegiance by transformational leadership.

How can church leaders shape and guide political processes to that end? Observation of practices currently seen in many churches suggests at least two diverse strategies. The understanding of leadership for fellowship building developed in this book suggests a third approach that lies between the other two and has some special emphases not present in either.

Pluralistic Partisan Politics

This strategy tries to leave as much decision making as possible close to all the members, thus presumably facilitating their control of what the congregation does. This thrust has been seen especially in mainline churches since World War II and is probably most fully developed among Presbyterians. Robert Worley describes it in *A Gathering of Strangers*[7] and gives it the name "pluralistic partisan politics." The pattern has striking similarities to the processes adopted by the national Democratic Party in the 1960s and '70s.

This approach to church politics recognizes that the constituent members of a congregation have different needs, interests,

_____
[7] Robert Worley, *A Gathering of Strangers* (Westminster Press, 1983).

and aspirations, and it assumes that they will commit themselves to the larger enterprise to the extent that they see their interests being met. Thus a church should have recurring occasions in which members can express their views and advocate their interests. Surveys and questionnaires can help represent and test the extent and strength of various views. Members should be encouraged to form coalitions to increase their power. The key provision is for decision making by the vote of a large group in which the various coalitions are well represented. The best outcome is that all feel that their voice has been heard and their needs are being addressed.

This summary is, of course, an oversimplification. The strengths of this approach are the way it binds the formal organization to the full membership and the way it provides for diversity. When a congregation has many gifted leaders and enough resources to meet a wide variety of interests, it can be quite successful at developing fellowship. But such a process represents fairly sophisticated politics and calls for adept political leadership on the part of the leaders—especially the pastor—who are responsible for the total work and welfare of the congregation.

Two related weaknesses are significant. One is the frequent absence of an overall vision to shape and direct the diversity—a vision reaching beyond commitment to democratic decision making. The parts often do not add up to a compelling whole that attracts new energy and participation. The other weakness, contributing to the first, is difficulty eliciting the transformed behaviors that build allegiance. The emphasis remains on members' commitments to the part that meets their individual interests. Rather than being transformational, church leadership is focused on the transactions of managing the political process.

Headship Authoritarian Relations

Opposite in many ways is a political strategy that looks for the definition of corporate commitment and direction not among the many members but in the overall leader. Authority is a key word (and one not heard much in the context of pluralistic partisan politics). The word itself means the source for something, usually something that has been done or should be done. Questions about authority relationships try to determine who or what is the source of preferences for actions to be taken.

This strategy focuses on the minister/leader as the center of

103

authority for church practices and programs. He (and it is usually a male in churches with this orientation) derives such authority from God by his interpretation of Scripture. This approach is often seen in fundamentalist churches with literal applications of Old Testament leadership patterns and New Testament headship references. It sometimes appears among individualistic pastors whose commitment to a specific mission, such as growth of the church or building a school, is so strong that little opposition is tolerated. Headship authority relations among Protestant churches can have striking similarities to the authority structure of Roman Catholicism, without the moderating effect of high-level authority within a hierarchy that transcends the local church.

According to this strategy, members will be moved beyond their own needs and interests—transformation will happen—by receiving clear Bible teaching, by being presented with a specific plan for churchwide involvement, and by being obedient to the authority behind that plan. Thus the goal for political leadership is for the leader to be unambiguous in detailed expectations and to be demanding in conformity. This can be an exclusionary strategy; those who are not willing to submit are usually encouraged to leave.

Strengths of this approach include the unified and often energetic action and outreach of a church whose members conform to this authority. Where accepted, authoritarian relations centered on the pastor can have a strong impact on the lives of participants and on moving them together in new directions. A desire for such forceful leadership is strong among many Christians.

Weaknesses include a propensity for friction and conflict as members measure their participation according to their assessment of the leader. The arrival of a new pastor can bring considerable turnover in membership. This strategy works best in small churches, where the pastor can develop a network of personal allegiances to support the intended authority relations. To lead with this approach in a large congregation, the pastor needs to be an exceptionally forceful preacher/teacher and shrewd politician. Unskilled imitation can have disastrous consequences for both pastor and congregation.

From the viewpoint of a theology of fellowship building as developed in previous chapters, this strategy has many limitations. It tends to view a church as an extension of the pastor rather than an expression of the fellowship. Often it sees the purpose for a church as being outside the body of Christ rather than the building of the Body. In exaggerated form, it can position the pastoral leader as accountable only to God and not also to the fellowship that is to be served.

Reinforced, Spiritually Committed Sharing

A political strategy for the fellowship envisioned here would lie somewhere between pluralistic partisan politics and headship authority relations. It would have to maintain an openness to the full diversity of needs and gifts present within a fellowship. Yet it needs to have a centralized decision-making group that is capable of fashioning and presenting a coherent and compelling vision, even when that leaves some interests unmet.

Incorporation—the building of allegiance to the larger body—is a result first of spiritual transformation of individuals through presentation of the Gospel that precipitates a loving response of commitment to fellowship sharing. It is not foremost a function of how well an individual's personal interests are met—though that may be a necessary starting point. Nor is it a function of submission to a leader's authority—though clear fellowship authority may need to be exercised at times. Growing commitment to the larger body happens through reinforced participation in the sharing activity of give-and-receive exchanges basic to fellowship sharing. Reinforcement comes when recognition and encouragement are offered for expressions of gifts of the Spirit brought by individuals to the fellowship.

Because spiritual gifts in a fellowship are so diverse, according to God's plan, the political process of giving them place and purpose within the fellowship is likely to be more responsive to needs and interests at hand than prescriptive about what should be done. Thus it is often imprecise. The pattern of effective decision making may shift from time to time and from congregation to congregation. Well-intentioned conflict is almost inevitable and can be seen as a not unwelcome sign of vitality. As with any grouping of people trying to assert their various perspectives and intentions, the political arrangements most appropriate are those that provide ways to resolve conflict, assure stability, and build agreement and coherence. Where there is doubt about how the political process should operate, control itself should not be the objective; building the fellowship should be.

The political role of the pastor/leader is likely to take various forms, even within the same denominational polity, because of differences in personality and in congregational needs. From the perspective of architectural leadership, the basic pastoral contribution (besides spiritual leadership) within the political process is to keep sights set on a Spirit-created, mutually accepted guiding vision that can be a rallying point for integrating shared efforts and resolving conflict. This sight setting is a distinctive role over against serving personally as the integrating source of authority, or as the designated mediator between special interest groups.

Dynamics suggestive of this approach are described by Frank R. Tillapaugh in *Unleashing the Church,* in which he discusses how ministries were stimulated and reinforced at Bear Valley Baptist Church in Denver.[8]

Exploration Topic B:
Allegiance-Building Communication

Communication is basic to building lasting allegiance. How leaders *talk* about the dynamics of fellowship can have a major impact on the cohesiveness and stability of that fellowship.

As usual, the apostle Paul is a good teacher. Note how his language contributes to allegiance. This can be done with insights generated by study of the New Testament from a sociologist's viewpoint. Warren A. Meeks is a good guide. In *The First Urban Christians* he inquires about the language practices and expressed sentiments that helped give those early fellowships cohesiveness. Cohesiveness is meant to describe the glue that held the members together—the allegiance they developed to their fellowship. Highlighting the use of languages and practices for that purpose in no way subtracts from the basic truth that was being described.

Meeks highlights first of all the language of belonging. That Paul concentrated on household groupings is significant. From the beginning he often underscored togetherness by using special identities for those first Christians: the saints, the holy ones, the elect, the called, those loved and known by God. He speaks of the members as if they were a family: brothers and sisters, children of God, children of mine, those adopted into the fellowship.

---

[8] Frank R. Tillapaugh, *Unleashing the Church* (Regal Books, 1978).

Paul's emphasis on distinctive beliefs also encouraged group coherence. In contrast to the polytheism of the culture around them, Paul points believers to the one God and Lord known by the Old Covenant people of God. It was precisely this single devotion to one God and their abhorrence of sharing his worship with that of others that gave the Jews their sense of being a unique people. Another example of what promoted a sense of distinctive identity is the faith in revelation made uniquely to believers. The significance of Jesus' death as God's Messiah and His resurrection was also a pivotal belief that effectively separated those first believers from the groups around them.

Meeks highlights how cohesiveness was promoted by special language that distinguishes the in-group from other groups. Untranslated Aramaic phrases like *Abba* and *marana tha* would almost certainly have been in-group identifiers. Similarly, specially loaded words were used to refer to those not in Christian fellowship, such as "the world," "the unbelievers," "the unrighteous."

From a sociological viewpoint, other Pauline emphases can be recognized for their allegiance-building impact. For Christians, circumcision would no longer be the clear sign of who was in the church and who was not. Other practices emerged to fulfill some of that boundary-setting function. Sexual purity was one; believers should keep themselves pure and not be like the "world." Believers should also not appear to practice idolatry by participating in the cults so prevalent around them. Of course, the Lord's Supper was a central practice in reinforcing cohesiveness; careful administration of it was also a boundary-defining act.

Again, that these basic Biblical beliefs can be recognized as having an impact on the cohesiveness of church life does not detract from their truthfulness. We can recognize Meeks' observations as underscoring the importance with which God views the community life of his church.[9]

---

[9] Warren A Meeks, *The First Urban Christians* (Yale University Press, 1982), pp. 84–103.

Chapter 7

Building a Full-Bodied Fellowship

First, we considered images for the *leaders:* carpenter, contractor, architect. Then there were images for the *followers:* lively stones, cornerstones, passive stones, inactive stones. Then we had images for *the sharing* between participants: exchanges, Seekers and Finders, role expectations. Now consider images for what all this adds up to. What are the leaders and followers trying to build? To consider such an overall image is to inquire about the nature of the Christian church itself.

Here is a general overview of four congregations.

St. Luke's Church is a mid-sized congregation in a mid-sized city. Founded in 1930, it has 500 members. Sunday attendance is about 200. The church celebrates the Lord's Supper every Sunday in a formal liturgical service. The sense of communion in the sacrament is emphasized. Once in a while the pastor also stresses the "communion of saints" in the "holy catholic church." There is a Bible class before the service and about 15 people attend. There is a "fellowship" hour after the service for which about 25 people stay. Activities during the week usually include several committee meetings and a pastor's confirmation class. The church is getting ready to raise dollars for a new organ and pew cushions.

First Church has a full calendar of activities throughout the week: a day-care center, Boy Scouts and Girl Scouts, two men's basketball teams, an aerobics class, a biweekly senior citizens gathering, monthly neighborhood meetings, and an evening weekly Bible study group. Because the congregation was once much larger, the building is bigger than it needs, and the church likes to make it available for the community. The building is maintained with income from an endowment. Sunday morning church attendance is usually between 80 and 100. What holds the members together now is the commitment to serve the community. They have a monthly session of dinner and discussion of a social issue.

Olive Fellowship is a group of young people that gathers weekly on Thursday evenings for Bible study and prayer in the home of Mrs. Jackson. She is an older lady and a member of the large Main Avenue Church nearby. The turnout has been as high as 70. Many are from Main Avenue Church, and others are students at the college in the area. Presently about 30 come, not always the same ones. The group is led by a team that does the planning. Two key members graduated last year, and the group has not been the same since. Leadership has not been resolved, and the team is getting discouraged by the low attendance. They have to decide whether to affiliate with a young-adult ministry at Main Avenue, try to keep it going as is, or let the group dissolve.

Christ Church has a membership of 300, and Sunday worship in two different styles has about 215, with three different choirs totaling 60 members. The Lord's Supper is celebrated weekly in alternate services. This church usually has about 15 small groups meeting weekly to share Scripture and prayer. Most meet in participants' homes. Sunday school for children has about a hundred in attendance and 15 teachers. There are three Sunday morning Bible classes with about 75 attending. Members participate in stocking a pantry with food to be distributed to people in the community who have need. Two committees concentrate on calling others, one for members who are hospitalized or in need and one to make fellowship visits with guests and others whom the church has identified for witnessing. The church helps support three missionaries in other countries.

The common element in these congregations is that each is a gathering of Christians trying to live out their understanding of church. They each have a different view of where they should be putting their energy and resources for the future.

Each is also a fellowship. That identifier will be given a fairly precise definition here. Each is a different kind of fellowship. Thus the building challenge for each is different. The preferred building project will become apparent.

St. Luke's Church is a *symbolic fellowship*. The members take their relationship with God seriously and focus their energies on worship. Their relationship with each other is celebrated in their frequent communion together at the Lord's Supper. But their relationship with each other typically does not extend beyond Sunday morning.

First Church is a *social fellowship*. They concentrate on the horizontal relationships with each other and with the community. They are anxious to live out the commitment to love one another. Their relationship with God is assumed but not often mentioned in the Sunday service.

The Olive Fellowship can be called an *occasional fellowship*. That they are a Christian fellowship is evident to anyone who comes. But they have not adopted a formal organization with rules and procedures. Their fellowship may or may not exist next year. The attractiveness of this informal group could fade in a few months just like it emerged somewhat spontaneously.

Christ Church is a *full-bodied fellowship*. About half of its members can be described as lively building stones (see chapter 3); they participate weekly in at least one other activity besides Sunday morning worship. The horizontal and vertical relationships are taken seriously, as expressed in the many different activities in worship, Bible study, service, and witnessing. Full-bodied can refer to the liveliness of this fellowship life as well as to the perception that the full body of Christ is emerging here.

The Fellowship as the Congregation

By now it should be apparent that church fellowship is more than sharing coffee and cookies after the service. And it is far more than dinner served in the "Fellowship Hall." Nor is it mainly a formal agreement between church bodies to "be in fellowship" with one another.

As used here, *fellowship* means all the basic interactions that a gathering of Christians has with God and with each other as they live their responses to God's call. It is the body of Christ incarnate in a particular location and the fundamental dynamic of church life. Fellowship is often viewed as merely one among many functions of a church; others are worship, nurture, service, and witnessing. Here it is not one of many but something fundamental to the expression of all the others. It describes the shared identity and energy that support and find expression in the full range of functions of church life. Although fellowship can describe all Christians worldwide, as in the "holy catholic church, the communion of saints," it will refer here to gathered Christians described as a congregation. That is the interpretation given to the apostle Paul's word *oikodomeō*, or "household building." The fellowship is the basic identity of a local congregation—a gathering, a specific community of Christians attempting to support each other's expression of their whole life in Christ.

The most evident Biblical source for this understanding is Acts 2:42, where we read that after Pentecost the first Christians "devoted themselves to the apostles' teaching and to *the* fellowship, to the breaking of bread and to prayer." The definite article used with "fellowship" means that it is a distinct entity. One interpretation is that "fellowship" was an early term for what later became "church" and was an initial identifier for the people who became known as Christians.

New Testament scholar Ralph Martin points out that other self-descriptive terms used in Acts were "the friends," "those of the way," and "the saints." He notes that devotion to the risen Lord was the hallmark of their way of life, and the lively, dynamic expression of what life in Christ meant comes into clear focus in appreciating all that is involved in "fellowship."[1]

"Fellowship" by derivation means being in partnership with others in a joint undertaking. "Communion" comes from the Latin. The Greek *koinōnia* perhaps most clearly identifies this concept as sharing something with someone. This definition points to the two dimensions of sharing—the "something" shared with the "somebody." Popular usage today often emphasizes the "somebodies" among whom sharing is taking place. New Testament usage tends to emphasize the "something" or the outside reality independent of human experience and independent of the shared experience.

Most clearly the something that is shared has the *vertical dimension* of relationship between God and people. In 1 Cor. 1:9 God calls His people "into fellowship" with His Son, Jesus Christ. Paul appeals to the Philippians to be like-minded if they have any encouragement from being with Christ and in "fellowship with the Spirit" (Phil. 2:1). He also thanks them for their partnership (*koinōnia*) in the Gospel (1:5). In 1 John 1:3 it is clear that our fellowship is with the Father and his Son. The epitome of Christian fellowship is the communion, the Lord's Supper. Speaking to the disunity of the Corinthians, Paul reminds them that they share (koinōneō) in the blood of Christ when they drink of the cup, and they share (the same verb form) in the body of Christ when they eat the bread (1 Cor. 10:16).

---

[1] Ralph Martin, *The Family and the Fellowship* (Eerdmans), p. 35.

The *horizontal dimension* of partnership between believers is emphasized in the passage that describes the fellowship of Acts 2:42. "All believers were together and had everything in common (koinē). Selling their possessions and goods, they gave to anyone as he had need" (vv. 44–45). Such giving and sharing between believers is highlighted in Paul's letter to the Romans about the poor among the saints in Jerusalem. "If the Gentiles have shared in the Jews' spiritual blessings, they owe it to the Jews to share with them their material blessings" (Rom. 15:27).

In assessing the Biblical use of *fellowship*, C. E. B. Cranfield notes that the vitality of this concept is indicated by all the Greek *syn*-compounds in the Greek New Testament with reference to the horizontal relationship: fellow servant, fellow worker, elect together, imitators together, to suffer with, to rejoice with, to find rest together, fitly framed together, built together, fellow partakers. He observes that many of these *syn*-compounds first occur in the New Testament, suggesting the newness and uniqueness of this Christian fellowship, togetherness far deeper than any mere camaraderie.[2]

In summary, "fellowship" means the local congregation understood as all gathered believers who share with each other all that God does for them.

Building a Fellowship to Be Full-Bodied

This focus on fellowship should not imply that it is the only or even the best image to use in thinking about the church. In his systematic study of images of the church in the New Testament, Paul S. Minear found 96 different Biblical images that range from such heavily used analogies as "body of Christ" and "people of God" to others that come as a surprise, like "pillar" and "buttress" (1 Tim. 3:15) or "fig tree" (Luke 13:6–9). The basic point is that God's church is much too great and mysterious to be captured by any one image.[3]

Which image of church one focuses on depends on what question is being considered. Here the question is, What are church leaders and members trying to build? *Fellowship* comes closest

---

[2] C. E. B. Cranfield, *Theological Wordbook of the Bible*, ed. Allen Richardson (New York: Macmillan, 1960), p. 82.

[3] Paul S. Minear, *Images of Church in the New Testament* (Westminster Press, 1960).

to describing a set of relationships that can be seen, fostered, shaped, and built. Particularly for administrative leadership, fellowship presents the most helpful image that defines the purpose for the externally visible, organizational dimension of the church. From an organizational perspective, church as fellowship enhances the heavily used image of the "body of Christ." The body image leads us to think of a tangible human body with Christ as its head and all the various members in place to exercise their gifts for the sake of the body. Yet the church as Christ's body is best appreciated from God's perspective, as He "combined the members of the body" (1 Cor. 12:24) and keeps them unified even in their diversity. How the parts of a body can be humanly combined is hard to envision short of transplant surgery. The image of fellowship understands the church more from the human perspective, suggesting ways in which a person can share with other believers because they all share in the presence of Christ through the Holy Spirit. Building the body can only be done metaphorically and remains abstract. Building fellowship can be as concrete and direct as bringing three people together to study God's Word and can be seen happening wherever church people gather.

To project an image for building, the concept of fellowship should have an adjective. To build implies making something different and improving it. "Full-bodied" seems an appropriate adjective to describe the kind of fellowship to which church builders can aspire in their leadership. A fellowship can strive to be full-bodied in its vertical relationships with God in the sense of participating in the fullness of God's presence in Christ and the Holy Spirit. It can aim to be full-bodied in terms of visible horizontal relationships involving most of the members. It can also build to become full-bodied in the sense of fostering a church life that supports the full, broad range of activities expected of Christians, like worship, nurture, service, and witnessing.

Other kinds of fellowship can be distinguished, and they present different building challenges. A *symbolic fellowship*, like St. Luke's congregation, takes seriously the vertical relationship of sharing in God's presence through Word and sacraments but does little to change or increase the sharing and caring of participants. Horizontal relationships are discussed more than performed, and when they are performed, it is only by a few. Here the church building challenge is to fill out the fellowship by keeping the central focus of strong worship while developing Sunday and

113

weekly occasions for interaction that will increase the fellowship sharing between many members.

Social fellowship, like that of First Church, describes a situation in which members share much of their time, energy, or resources (like a physical building) in horizontal relationships with each other and with people of the community. But their sharing in God's power and promises is assumed and only minimally sought. Some social fellowships may be no different from the city Elks Club. Here the church building challenge is to confront members more clearly with God's full Word and to extend their vision to cultivate personal spiritual development.

Occasional fellowship, like that of Olive Fellowship, describes a gathering of believers that stays quite informal and happens only once in a while, such as the Thursday evening group presented earlier. There is an absence of stable organization that can assure continuity, establish leadership, and resolve conflict. The first building question is whether this should be the primary fellowship for those involved, or is it mostly a fellowship event of an established church? If it is to be a congregation by itself, the building challenge is to develop a formal organizational structure to define it, facilitate its continuity, and be responsible for its resources while it maintains "order."

Is fellowship really a big enough concept to include all that church leaders expect churches to be and do today? A common reaction to this emphasis is that it is too much an inward-looking image, concentrating on the church members themselves. Churches should be outward-looking, to the service and witnessing that is to be done among those outside the church. Churches are called to be selfless, not selfish.

This criticism is certainly appropriate from leaders who hear the term *fellowship* in its popular, rather superficial sense. The church social functions of togetherness are typically far from outward-looking. But they are hardly the best reference point for the theologically encompassing sense of fellowship envisioned here. Believers responding to God's call to follow him will want to support each other in the broad range of Christian actions, from worship to personal growth in God's Word, witnessing the Gospel to others, and caring for and serving fellow humans in whatever condition. Conveying this understanding is the purpose for adding the adjective "full-bodied." A full-bodied fellowship incarnates at a particular time and place the body of Christ in all its fullness.

The Fellowship and the Church Organization

Building fellowship can be an organizational task. But the local church fellowship and the local church organization are not the same things, even though they are easily confused. Keeping the two separate, at least conceptually, is important.

To summarize the points that follow: Knowing the differences between the church as fellowship and the church as organization enables church leaders more clearly to recognize where the distinct divine nature is that makes church special and unlike any other human shared endeavor. God's special presence is in the Word-centered event interactions of the fellowship. Fostering, protecting, and enhancing that presence and those interactions is the assigned task for the organizational dimension that a congregation develops. The organization is secondary; the Christ-centered fellowship is primary. This should be a freeing insight for organizational leaders, because if the fellowship is the focal point of God's presence, leaders can feel free to develop the organizational dimension of the church as creatively as possible.

These seemingly simple points touch on church leadership understandings that are anything but obvious. Prevalent misunderstandings generate many of the difficulties congregations find themselves in while trying to live out their necessary nature as a church of God.

Several images can help illustrate the distinction. The church as formal organization is similar in many ways to the physical church building within which church life occurs. Both are usually carefully planned structures meant to facilitate interactions. But both are one or several steps removed from the real identity of the church.

The organizational dimension of a congregation is like the city government of a community. The formal government usually consists of only a fraction of the people and activities that make up the basic community. The purpose of the governmental function is to support and enrich the life of that particular community.

The church as formal organization involves a structure of committees, boards, officers, duties, staff assignments, job descriptions, legal ownership of property, constitutions, etc. Members go to meetings at church once or twice a month—or more often. This is what administrative leaders spend so much of their time tending. Unfortunately, church organization is what most Christians in congregations of long-established denominations are accustomed to seeing when they look at the church.

Many church leaders today see the problems of a congregation as not having enough organization. This is often a legitimate concern. But a greater problem with many congregations is that they make too much of their church organization and wind up misdirecting much of their effort.

Both organization and fellowship fit within the larger category of a structure, a pattern of relationships between people interacting with each other. All but the most temporary groups will develop patterns of who typically interacts with whom, how often this happens, and who usually initiates interaction and determines its content. Such patterns constitute the structure among participants in any set of relationships.

The presence of structure in and of itself is not the same as *organization*, at least as this key term is understood and used in modern organization theory. *Organization* describes a structure of interaction that is rationally planned, explicitly prescribed, and accepted among participants acting according to specific roles and rules. This focus is clarified by the designation "formal organization," which is on one end of a continuum of structure. The other end is "informal" structure, in which the patterns develop without careful forethought and deliberate agreement. The usual reason for introducing formal organization into interactions is to stabilize relationships and to assure that certain purposes are accomplished within them. Such formalized structure can exist alongside or be grafted onto an informal structure that involves most of the same people but does so in relationships that may also be casual and spontaneous, spilling beyond the boundaries and roles of the interactions prescribed in the formal organization. Indeed, without organization, boundaries for relationships are hard to identify. The dividing line between a fellowship and its formal organization is not precise. There are usually many more informal interactions going on than formal. A fellowship can and often does exist without much of a formal organization, but a healthy church organization cannot exist for long without the underlying spiritual fellowship that it is trying to express.

116

Perhaps the simplest way to make the distinction and to convey its importance is in terms of primary and secondary relationships. Sociologically, the primary group exists for its own sake without serving as a means to some other end. Examples are a family, a household, or a close-knit neighborhood. A family does not have to justify its presence. It is a basic unit of society that simply exists for its own sake. So also a fellowship of believers, with a broad range of often minimally defined, changing, eventlike relationships, is the basic unit of the church. *The Family and the Fellowship* is the title of one study of fellowship.[4]

Secondary relationships must justify their existence in terms of some end to which they are a means. They exist to serve some primary relationships. Formal organization, with its rationally preplanned, explicitly accepted roles and rules, is a set of such secondary relationships. The surest way to determine the presence of secondary, organizational interaction is to look for a structure that is incorporated with a written constitution and bylaws. Not all formal organizations have a constitution, but all churches with a constitution have secondary relationships with a purpose beyond themselves. Organization remains a tool for accomplishing something else.

What is the purpose to be served by the secondary, formal organization? Many church constitutions say that the objective of the congregation is to preach the Gospel and administer the sacraments, and indeed these are the visible marks of the church. But this is still not a sufficient statement of purpose, because preaching the Gospel and administering the sacraments are themselves means to an end. State the objective for these central church activities and you have the purpose of the formal organization. Church preaching and/or organizing are done to care for, expand, intensify, challenge, and protect the body of Christ congregated in fellowship at a specific place. From that fellowship some participants accept secondary and additional roles in its formal organization. The institution remains a part of a fellowship just like any other interaction of members. But it cannot displace the fellowship or present itself as the church in the fullest sense.

Clarifying primary and secondary relationships accomplishes at least two things. It keeps the special divine mystery of God's presence located in Christ-centered primary fellowship and

---

[4] Ralph Martin, *The Family and the Fellowship* (Erdmans).

thereby releases the formal secondary organization from somehow having to be exempt from the dynamics of other human organizational arrangements. The distinction also means that there is no one organizational arrangement that is more faithfully God-given than another.

This understanding gives church leaders opportunity to change, rearrange, or be as innovative as necessary in organizing the congregation to build the fellowship and further its welfare. The organization remains a human arrangement that can be chosen as rationally as any other corporate form in society.

The Misunderstanding of the Church

Why bother forcing the issue of informal and formal relationships? For one reason, because for centuries the church has been misunderstood. Christian leaders looked at institutional structure and called that the church. Then they were left trying to figure out what makes it different from any other institution or formal organization in society. Where does its divine nature fit in?

All Christians would agree that there is something special about the church as an expression of God's presence. Is the distinctiveness found in the physical building or the vestments? Of course not, although these symbols can help point to God's presence. Is it a special identity for its leaders or a special polity that has unique principles of organization? Now we are getting closer to what many Christians would identify as special. Yet, except for their different titles and names, the leadership arrangements and organizational principles seem much like those that can be found in a study of general organizational behavior, and it is hard to say that only one polity is the true one. Is the special characteristic of the church found in the words that are spoken? True, where God's Word is spoken, special things happen. But there must be more to the church, since the Word is also read and heard in contexts that are somewhat removed from what most believers consider to be the church.

We are looking for the "mystery" of the church that makes it unlike any other group of people. That mystery of God's special presence is found in the lives and interactions of believers, his children. Their relationships usually extend far beyond the relatively few aspects of interaction with which the institution concerns itself. Among believers in whom Christ lives, whose lives

118

God changes, and who are led by the Spirit to share with one another—there is something special, the mystery.

When Luther and Calvin looked at the church of their day, they could only see an institution, and they knew that more was involved. They differentiated between the visible church (the institution) and the invisible church made up of all who believe, wherever they are. Yet the living believers were quite visible. The bonds holding them together could not be recognized apart from the institution.

With the rise of an economic understanding of the legal identity of a corporation, later generations began to differentiate between *Gemeinschaft* (community) and *Gesellschaft* (corporation). For instance, the people who live, work, and shop within the boundaries of Pasadena are a community. Their exact number would be hard to determine at any given time. Some of them—only a small fraction—take on additional relationships within the incorporated governmental entity called the City of Pasadena. Those who are in some rationally specified, explicitly defined relationship with others could be determined on any given day.

In terms of the church, the fellowship is the community, and the institution amounts to a second set of relationships involving those who serve the larger body. The criterion for determining how effectively a city government or a church institution operates is the welfare of the primary community.

Theologian Emil Brunner caused a stir in ecumenical circles with his 1951 publication of *The Misunderstanding of the Church*.[5] He argued forcefully that the outwardly visible institutional church is not really the New Testament *ecclēsia*, and therefore to argue about which is the true church is beside the point. Brunner was basically correct. But he went too far in his distinction, because the institutional church is made up of some of the same people who are in the fellowship. He did not have the conceptual framework to understand institutions as a set of specialized formal relationships existing alongside and among the fellowship relationships.

Some theologians, such as Jürgen Moltmann, distinguish between church as event and church as institution. The real church is found in the events, or "happenings." The institution is the set

---

[5] Emil Brunner, *The Misunderstanding of the Church* (Westminster Press, 1951).

of arrangements that church people make to assure and protect future events of interaction with God and others.[6] His distinction gives added weight to the emphasis here on fellowship as event and interaction.

Designing the Secondary Organization of the Church

An organization can be seen, understood, and developed in several ways. For recent overviews of organizational theory, see especially Lee Bolman and Terrence Deal, *Modern Approaches to Understanding and Managing Organizations*[7] or Gareth Morgan's *Images of Organization.*[8]

Two of the most basic and practical ways will be developed in chapter 9, which will distinguish between seeing participants as parts or as plants. Seeing people as parts to be assembled happens when the organization is regarded as a machine of ideal positions and relationships into which the participants are to be fitted. Seeing people as plants to be planted, watered, and pruned comes from viewing organization as a garden with life sprouting here and there and needing cultivation.

The most general and comprehensive approach is called *systems theory*. This envisions organization as deliberate, rationally planned interventions into an existing set of relationships among participants. A system can be defined as the presence of many different components or participants that act in interdependent relationships and that fit together as a whole greater than the sum of its parts. Even considering secular literature, there is no better description of a system than the one Paul gives in the image of the body of Christ:

> *Now the body is not made up of one part but of many. . . .*
> *God has arranged the parts in the body, every one of them, just*
> *as he wanted them to be. . . . The eye cannot say to the hand,*
> *"I don't need you!" And the head cannot say to the feet, "I don't*
> *need you!" . . . If one part suffers, every part suffers with it;*

---

[6] Jürgen Moltmann, *The Church in the Power of the Spirit* (Harper and Row, 1977), p. 333.

[7] Lee G. Bolman and Terrence E. Deal, *Modern Approaches to Understanding and Managing Organizations* (Jossey Bass, 1984).

[8] Gareth Morgan, *Images of Organization* (Sage, 1986).

if one part is honored, every part rejoices with it. (1 Cor. 12:14, 18, 21, 26)

The fellowship is the body of Christ congregated in one place. The Holy Spirit gives the body life by bringing believers together in the basic interactions of fellowship sharing. Although still only an informal structure, a fellowship is a system in which the sum is greater than the parts.

The need for formal organization arises to the extent that problems occur within the fellowship and keep it from accomplishing its purposes. If there were no potential problems, there would be no need for formal organization. Church organization is best seen as carefully defined assignments and relationships aimed at strengthening or changing components of the larger entity that are weak, shifting, or the source of repeated conflict. The task of organizational leadership is to intervene when some components within the fellowship are no longer functioning effectively or when changes from outside threaten the existing balance among fellowship members.

The leadership challenge is to guide adaptations to change by continually clarifying basic God-given purposes and by interpreting changes for the participants so that they can respond sensibly and continue to fulfill the purpose that brought them into the fellowship.

Systems theory is mentioned here to reaffirm that the secondary organization must fit the primary fellowship. The right amount of formal organization is only as much as is needed. Churches can be underorganized or overorganized. When under organized, the fellowship can deteriorate because basic interaction problems, like succession of leadership or resolution of conflict, are not solved. When overorganized, the fellowship can also deteriorate as primary, Spirit-led interactions are crowded out by the busyness of organizational routines that have become ends in themselves. The effectiveness of a church organization is measured by the overall welfare of its primary fellowship—that is, how well the participants interact in sharing the Word and in helping each other live out the many necessary dimensions of the new life in Christ.

Administration is essentially the work of developing and guiding the formal organization of a church so that it can better shape and protect the church's Christ-centered fellowship interactions and events. Its overall function in a congregation can be expressed in the following diagram:

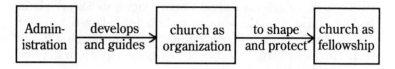

| Admin-istration | develops and guides | → | church as organization | to shape and protect | → | church as fellowship |

Much church leadership can be exercised directly with the fellowship in all sorts of primary events, like Bible study or witnessing. Administrative leadership is a step away from the primary, because it deals with the secondary relationships of organization. Understandably, it is less exciting and fulfilling for many pastors, who prefer other leadership roles than that of administrator. Yet a lasting fellowship will need a formal organization, and a church organization needs leadership oriented to keep it tuned to its God-given spiritual purposes. Administrative leadership has too much potential for both good and bad impact to be bypassed in pursuit of other forms of ministry.

Governance and Ministry Structures

The design of a church organization will be improved by recognizing two fundamental purposes that call for different structures. One is governance, which needs a structure through which representatives of the fellowship can resolve leadership issues and make major resource allocation decisions on behalf of the fellowship. The other is ministry, which needs a structure through which the direct doers of ministry can be guided and supported in their primary acts of ministry.

The governance structure is usually the most visible and easily recognized formal organization in churches. It consists of the councils, boards, and elected officers that are charged with overseeing the welfare of the organization, assuring that everything be done "in a fitting and orderly way" (1 Cor. 14:40). These groups function as representatives of the larger body. The positions and relationships are usually carefully prescribed in the constitution. In some denominations this is called the polity structure.

The ministry structure is the pattern of relationships among the workers of a congregation, such as Sunday school teachers, visitation teams, potluck organizers, ushers, or leaders of various kinds of activity groups. This organization can often be loose and informal, with interactions taking place only as the doers need support to get the tasks done. Or it can be more formalized, with appointed team or group leaders who themselves become a group that needs to be led and supported. In larger churches these second-level group leaders might gather occasionally as a higher-level group to improve their activities and relationships. Thus the ministry structure can be expanded to as many areas and levels as seems helpful.

Recognizing the difference in purpose helps to ensure that the appropriate structure can be rationally planned and the right kind of participants involved. Governance is best accomplished through a structure designed to make decisions about authority, resource allocation, and overall coordination, much like the legislative branch of a city or state. The purpose of this structure is to ensure that the needs and interests of the larger fellowship are recognized and dealt with. It is not the best structure for actually implementing the plans, because the participants may not see themselves as workers or may not be gifted for such work. A common example of such confusion is the elders of a church, who along with oversight duties are often expected to visit members with special needs but who frequently do little of this ministry and feel guilty about it.

Actual hands-on ministry is best accomplished through a structure that matches willing workers with needs as directly and quickly as possible. It is similar to the executive branch of government. Someone who is ready to do a ministry of visitation should receive the necessary preparation and regularly be given names of people to visit. The best supporting structure keeps a worker in contact with a leader who can provide training, resources, and encouragement. Expecting the worker or even the leader to attend a monthly governance committee meeting may be adding a burden that could become an unnecessary source of frustration. Participants in the ministry structure could be considered as staff, whether or not they are paid. In this sense, a church might have a staff of hundreds.

Applying systems thinking to designing the secondary structure of church organization would yield this advice: Keep the governance structure as minimal as possible to provide good representation but to take no more time or energy than necessary. Put more leadership effort into expanding a streamlined ministry structure that can keep gifted and willing workers engaged in their ministry with as much support and as little interference as possible.

This design distinction is more useful the larger a congregation becomes. Smaller congregations often do not have enough willing members to distinguish two structures; committees must serve the dual purpose of representation and implementation.

As churches become larger, the ministry structure requires increasing attention—more than can consistently be given by volunteers. Such churches need to consider adding paid staff to administer the various ministry efforts if they want to continue building the fellowship. Poor distinction of ministry from governance structures and insufficient staff leadership are basic reasons why congregations level off in their membership and activities.

Exploration Topic A: A Mutual Benefit Association

The significance of understanding the church as a fellowship becomes more apparent by noting a distinction offered by Peter M. Blau and W. Richard Scott.[9] They ask who is the prime beneficiary of an organization's effort and see four alternatives that point toward four types of organization: (1) a mutual benefit association for the benefit of the members, (2) a business concern for the owners or managers, (3) a service organization for clients, or (4) a commonweal organization (like government) for the public at large.

It may be proper to think of church organization as being for the benefit of its owner if we assume that the owner is God. And it undoubtedly happens that some human church leaders start thinking that a congregation exists for their benefit. But to think of church as a business is disturbing.

The church as a governmental commonweal organization would have the public at large as its beneficiaries. Presumably it would promote special values in society, like justice and equal rights. This view of the purpose of the church has been especially

---

[9] Peter M. Blau and W. Richard Scott, *Formal Organizations: A Comparative Approach* (San Francisco: Chandler, 1962), p. 38.

attractive in recent decades characterized by political activism in many mainline denominations.

The church would be a service organization when it is seen existing for the benefit of clients or specific persons outside the church. This perspective can be found among mission-minded leaders who focus so much on witnessing to the lost that other purposes for church life are left in the background.

The view of fellowship building developed here would see the church as congregations existing for the benefit of their members. The formal organization of a church serves its purpose best when it is patterned like a mutual benefit association. It exists to guide and protect the members and to build them into a fuller fellowship.

This view often meets strong resistance. It appears to some as selfish and lacking in concern for missionary activity. But such an attitude develops only when the formal mutual benefit association of the church is weak or unfaithful in serving its fellowship. The Christian life has many dimensions, often summarized as worshiping God, growing in his Word, and caring for and witnessing to others. A faithful secondary church organization will want to be sure that these dimensions are successfully pursued in the fellowship. When the church organization plans a service project, the objective is not just to get people served but to give opportunity for members in the fellowship to live out that dimension of their faith. The same is true of witnessing. The aim is not just to bring someone into the fellowship but to have the fellowship experience that dimension of its faith. Only as the organization sees itself stimulating and guiding all the dimensions of Christian living, not just a few, can those active in the organization build a full-bodied fellowship.

Exploration Topic B: Models of the Church

There are alternative ways to view organization. What are the alternatives for how to see and think about church?

Avery Dulles, a Jesuit, provides a stimulating overview of five different ecclesiologies in *Models of the Church*.[10] A model is a simplified version of what it represents, highlighting features

---

[10] Avery Dulles, *Models of the Church* (Image Books, 1974).

that seem important for one purpose or another. Dulles presents five models:

the church
as institution
as mystical communion
as sacrament
as herald
as servant

There is considerable tradition behind a Roman Catholic view of the church as an *institution*, a visible organization with rights and powers assigned to its officers. It exists for the benefit of its members, whom it serves by instructing them in the truths they need for salvation. Dulles points out that this theory has only a weak basis in Scripture or early church history. It accentuates clericalism and reduces the laity to passive recipients.

His second model is church as *mystical communion*. Again, *communion* is a Latin word for the notion of fellowship. It is mystical because it is the body of Christ. The community is held together by the graces and gifts of the Holy Spirit. Dulles identifies several weaknesses of this approach. It leaves some obscurity about the relationships between the spiritual and the visible dimensions of the church. It also fails to give Christians a clear sense of their identity or mission. There is also a tension between the church as a network of friendly interpersonal relations and the church as a mystical communion.

This model corresponds almost exactly with the theology of fellowship building developed here. Dulles' criticism also seems appropriate. As acknowledged, the line between the spiritual and the visible dimensions *is* hard to draw. Yet conceptually the distinction is basic. The sense of mission does remain less clearly focused because all of the Christian life becomes the concern of the church. And unfortunately, the word *fellowship* has become trivialized as a set of friendly relations. Yet the full Scriptural concept is too important to let a superficial use denigrate the profound meaning and implications for church leadership.

Dulles himself prefers the model of church as *sacrament*. It is a way to bring the visible and mystical dimensions of the church together. A sacrament is a sign of grace realizing itself, according to Dulles, and a church becomes like a sacrament when it binds people together in grace by a visible expression. A weakness is that this approach does not preach well because it is technically

126

sophisticated. Dulles points out that this view is gaining adherence among Catholic theologians but has found little response in Protestant thought.

The church as *herald* has found ready acceptance among Protestants. The church is essentially a herald of Christ's lordship and of the future kingdom. It is the *ecclesia*, those who are called out, and the event of proclaiming is the definitive characteristic of the church. Although this view gives a clear sense of mission, Dulles sees its basic limitation as making little provision for the human institutional form of the church and its continuation as a community. He also worries that it focuses too exclusively on witness to the neglect of action.

The church as *servant* exists for all people the world over who hear from it a word of comfort or encouragement or obtain a respectful hearing or receive some material help in their time of need. The church does not exist for itself or have any privileged standing in society; it becomes relevant by what it contributes to the world in terms of the pursuit of justice, alleviation of poverty, or elimination of racism. Dulles finds a serious objection to this popular modern view in the lack of any direct Biblical foundation for this type of service role for the church. How such a servant church relates to the kingdom of God also remains unclear. The emphasis on the supernatural is easily lost.

These models are not necessarily mutually exclusive. They emerge because of emphases that are appropriate for questions and circumstances that theologians want to address. The context in this study is the local congregation, and the question is how leaders can be more effective there. The church as fellowship or mystical communion serves that purpose well. It is reassuring that there is a distinct ecclesiology to support this emphasis.

Chapter 8 _____

Shaping the Vision

The building committee of Christ Church was meeting with architect Sylvia Pitman, whom they had engaged to help in their planning. The committee consisted of three elders, two trustees, and Pastor William Baumeister.

One major issue was whether or not to relocate the church to another part of town. That decision in turn depended on how much additional space they could add to the existing building. Underlying these questions was the vision of how large they saw this congregation becoming in the future and what ministries they would emphasize.

Christ Church has 300 members, with 215 usually attending on Sunday morning. For most of its 25-year history, the congregation had fit comfortably into a sanctuary built 20 years ago. They started a second service 10 years ago. Attendance at that time was usually about 50 in the early service and 100 in the late. Three years after Pastor Baumeister arrived, the sanctuary was usually filled almost to its capacity of 150 in the second service with 65 in the first.

The committee felt excited about the growth they were experiencing. Some wanted to think big. Others felt almost overwhelmed by the cost that more building would entail. Sylvia Pitman outlined a relatively modest project of extending the south wall out and seating 50 more people. This unfortunately would entail the loss of eight parking spaces, and parking was now becoming a problem.

Some on the committee expressed concern about the lack of space that they were facing because of growing Sunday school and Bible classes. One elder thought that might not be so important because the trend now was to have members meet in small home groups during the week. Another thought that a ministry to provide day care was becoming more important. A day care center could also be used on Sunday for classes.

Tonight they were talking about the worship center. One trustee offered his solution: just tell more people to come to the early service. Miss Pitman asked the group how the worship would "feel" with the south wall extension. No one was enthused about it. Then one of the members asked Pastor Baumeister what he would like to see.

Proceeding cautiously, Pastor Baumeister described his hope for the future. He noted that they had reached the "200 barrier" and would probably experience no more growth if they did not address the space problem. He could see God blessing them with 400 in attendance in five years; the potential was definitely there. As far as worship goes, he would like to dream about a semicircular room with a free-standing altar in the front. It might also be wise to provide for a future addition, too.

As others reacted, the discussion came back to the point they had reached several times already. They cannot stay at this location and grow much more. Miss Pitman reminded them that the basic question they had to answer was how large they wanted to become. She suggested that the group think, talk, and pray about that in the next several weeks. If they would give her a number for seating capacity, she could sketch out several alternatives for accommodating that, assuming that they would move to another location.

Pastor Baumeister agreed that that was the basic question. He wondered whether they were ready to answer it. Maybe it was too early to talk to an architect. Perhaps they should get some help to think through the issue of what they wanted to be.

Strategic Planning

Whether they realize it or not, this group of church people is engaged in strategic planning. They are making decisions about what to do now that will determine much of their future identity. They are ready to commit resources to actions in order to achieve a few goals among the many they could pursue.

In the last several decades, strategic planning has emerged as a central emphasis in business management. This specialized form of planning tries to shape the overall direction of an organization for 5 or 10 years into the future. Other planning activity can be short-range, concentrating on what to do next week, or medium-range, considering how to get ready for the next year. *Strategy* is a military term. Its Greek root refers to the generalship of an army. Most military officers take care of tactical implementation of an overall plan that they are given. The general has to establish the master plan. Specifically, military strategy deals with decisions about objectives to strive for, where troops should be positioned, what their assignments are, and when to move. General Douglas MacArthur was recognized as a master strategist in his approach to World War II in the Pacific.

A simple definition of strategy is the leader's determination that specific available resources will be applied to addressing specifically recognized opportunities to accomplish clearly identified goals. Such planning is not simply making decisions about what to do five years from now. No one can know the future. Decisions can only be made about actions at hand. But church planners, like other institutional planners, can arrive at an opinion about the probability of several different outcomes. They can decide which outcome they would prefer and what they can do now to prepare for it.

In the early part of this century Max Weber pointed out three basic approaches that societies can take in getting fundamental decisions made for their cooperative endeavors. One is reliance on tradition; people can just keep doing what they have done in the past. If the future is similar to the past, this approach is useful. A second approach is to rely on decisions that will be made by a charismatic leader. Weber was among the first to use "charisma" in this context; he meant it in a more general sense than is commonly used in the church today. The people in effect entrust their future to a captivating leader and are ready to go where he or she leads. A third approach is rational decision making that relates cause to effect and chooses among several known alternatives.

When people rely on tradition, their explanation for doing one thing versus another is that it always has been done that way. Relying on a charismatic leader means doing whatever that leader wants. In rational decision making, specific reasons are cited for choosing a particular course of action as the best among the known alternatives.

For most of its history the Christian church has relied on charismatic or traditional decision making. Jesus Christ was, humanly speaking, a charismatic leader with his disciples. Peter, Paul, and Martin Luther were charismatic leaders who left substantial imprints on the decisions of their followers. But within several generations of major formative events, tradition usually settled in. Weber called these dynamics a "routinization of charisma." For most of church history, the future looked much like the past, and tradition was a good guide.

As futurologists like to point out, in this century the rate of change far outpaces that of previous centuries, stimulated by constant improvements in technology. Churches cannot escape such change happening among the members or in the community and culture around them. That is why they are increasingly relying on rational decision making, often aided by consultants who can point out new alternatives and broaden their understanding of consequences.

Church leaders who are feeling their way into this approach often express concerns about faithfulness. God alone can determine the future, and they may feel that it is presumptuous for His followers to pretend to do it. And it *is* presumptuous to try to determine the future, but that is not what rational planning does. It can only affect current decisions, but it does so in anticipation of future outcomes. The future of the church in general and of a congregation in particular depends squarely on the movement of the Holy Spirit. Church leaders can consider how the Spirit might be best able to move among people today and try to determine what they might do in their own setting.

A Vision for Excellence: Reaching for the Height

Planning is a rather prosaic way of talking about the future; it is usually not very exciting. Nor will it become exciting until it becomes part of a compelling vision.

An idea becomes a vision for church building when it is a shared view that pulls out from gathered believers new or increased energy for building up the body of Christ. A hope or view of what to build is not a compelling church vision if it is held only by the pastor and a few leaders and is not shared by most members. The energy and commitment of the large group of people must provide the momentum to keep building.

The first Pentecost was certainly a time of excitement and vision. Here was how the apostle Peter explained what was going on, quoting the prophet Joel:

"In the last days, God says,
  I will pour out my Spirit on all people.
Your sons and daughters will prophesy,

your young men will see visions,
your old men will dream dreams.
Even on my servants, both men and women,
I will pour out my Spirit in those days,
and they will prophesy." (Acts 2:17–18)

The Holy Spirit will grant a shared compelling vision where and when He wills. Churches can work to get ready for His movement. The best way, of course, is to stay close to God's Word. Beyond that, churches will be readier when people spend time together talking and thinking about what else or what more they could be doing with the resources God gives them—that is, seeing visions and dreaming dreams.

Here is a way to state the challenge: In Eph. 4 Paul notes God's gift of leaders (apostles, prophets, evangelists, and pastors and teachers). They are gifts God sends "to prepare God's people for works of service, so that the body of Christ may be built up until we all reach unity in the faith and in the knowledge of the Son of God and become mature, attaining to the whole measure of the fullness of Christ" (vv. 12–13).

Consider the last phrase. Its Greek syntax is tortuous. The Today's English Version (Good News Bible) is most helpful. The purpose for building the body is that people be united in faith and knowledge. That in turn is to enable them to become mature people. Now comes the key phrase: "reaching to the very height of Christ's full stature" (Eph. 4:13 TEV).

Let the slogan for church building be "reaching to the very height." Another word for reaching high is "excelling." Leader/builders can constantly ask, Where do we want to reach? How do we want to excel? There will always be more of Christ's full stature to reach for. A church will always have something more to do and somewhere to reach. Striving for excellence in building a fellowship is a constant challenge for leaders trying to build the body of Christ.

The other purpose is to become mature. People usually become mature after a certain amount of growth and experience. We generally assume that when they are mature, they have arrived at what they are going to be and will stay that way for most of the rest of their lives. Congregations can also think of themselves as mature and beyond growth. But the standard is not human opinion about church maturity. It is the pursuit of the height of Christ's full stature.

The question for any congregation, large or small, is, Which height or heights will they seek? Where do they want to excel? When they have reached as far as they can in one area, there are always more dimensions of church life to build up.

The answer to the question of where to reach high comes best when, after hearing and studying God's Word, church leaders prayerfully get specific about the building challenge they want to strive for, should God grant them this blessing. The best way to get specific is to use a strategic planning approach.

Christ Church was deeply into strategic planning with the need to make specific decisions about the future they hope to prepare for. Most church leaders readily understand the need to pin down the future expectations for seating capacity in the sanctuary, functional uses of all sorts of other rooms, and more recently, the amount of parking they need. They also readily understand the need for getting specific about resources—mostly money and time. Sooner or later they get the dreams matched with the estimate of resources and make their commitment. Cutting back on a project is hard once it has started. Bankers will tell you that churches have an excellent track record of repaying loans. Once committed to a vision of church life in a new building, church leaders will work hard to get the project completed.

The challenge in fellowship building is to make visions of where God wants us to reach in church life as visible and tangible as constructing a physical building so that everyone can work as hard as they would for a physical building campaign. Visions of how to reach higher in worship, nurture, service, or witness must flow from a theological understanding of God's call to the congregation. But visions must also be interpreted in terms of numbers of people and groups, kinds of activities, hours and dollars involved, and other descriptions that are understandable to most members.

At Christ Church, the leaders will set a long-term strategy in their meetings one way or another. Remaining as is would limit the membership growth to just a bit more than it is now. There may be valid reasons to do that. The church may envision other heights to reach for. Whether to build fellowship is not the issue; that is the task of church leaders. Where to reach and how to get there are the driving questions.

SWOTS Analysis

The study of strategy is basic to what a modern business school does. Churches can learn something from their approach. A strategy course in a business school would usually rely heavily on a SWOT analysis, or something like it. The usual format is for a new, real-life case and a new analysis each week. The analysis is done around a SWOT outline.

For churches, a final S can be added:

Strengths Weaknesses Opportunities Threats Satisfactions

In a group planning session, these words can be written across a large surface with one column for each. In discussion, entries are made under each. *Strengths* and *weaknesses* refer to the resources a local church has. These can be member commitment and attitudes, leadership capabilities, strong personalities, remembered history of success or conflict as well as facilities and finances. *Opportunities* are needs that a church can address (or heights to reach for), both in the general community and among the membership. *Threats* are negative consequences that a church will face if current conditions remain as they are. A hole in the roof is a tangible threat to the building that must be fixed. A changing neighborhood can also be a threat for a church that does not want to change. Of course, a changing neighborhood can also be an opportunity for a new ministry.

A *strategy* is the rational determination of which organizational resources will be committed to which opportunities (needs) to accomplish which goals. The first two columns—strengths and weaknesses—are the resources. The second two—opportunities (or needs) and threats—are the next step in an analysis.

Finally come the goals to be considered. Remember that formalized organizational action must serve some goal to justify this special effort. Experience with pastors leads to the conclusion that talking about goals often prompts descriptions of desired outcomes that remain too theologically abstract to facilitate effective planning. Better is "satisfactions to offer," which usually elicits a clearer, more specific response. Hence, the final S in the SWOTS format.

Identifying the satisfactions to be offered determines the goals for committing a church's resources. The question is, What will our church life look like if the intended efforts are effective?

How many and which people would be doing what activities, where, and how often? If a video camera were aimed at the congregation at the end of the planning period, what would the participants be doing?

The significance of satisfactions in individual motivation was discussed in chapter 4. Implications for Christian church life were developed in chapter 5 with the focus on helping seekers become finders—that is, offering something that will satisfy specific needs of specific people wanting to act on them.

The Strategic Planning Guide on page 136 offers a summary of categories for considerations that go into developing a strategic plan for a church. It can be used to focus attention on rational steps that lead to decisions about committing resources.

This guide has five parts that call for identification and evaluation through extensive discussion.

I. Identification of SWOTS

A SWOTS analysis focuses attention on the
—Strengths and Weaknesses of the resources
—Opportunities and Threats of needs to address
—Satisfactions that can be offered

> *"Satisfactions" is a better description of goals for churches because it typically elicits clearer, more specific descriptions of intended outcomes.*
>
> *Good strategic planning will describe how many and which people will be doing what activities, where and how often at the end of a planning period. This is basic to the vision.*

II. Evaluation of alternative combinations according to their importance, feasibility and fit with a congregation.

III. Choice of one combination and thereby selection of a basic strategy that will be followed in guiding future organizational effort.

IV. Determination of which possible actions will be deferred and not pursued at this time. Without such a decision there is really no strategy. "To decide" literally means to cut off. Something has to be left behind in order to focus energy effectively.

V. Provision for implementation by determining which programs should be developed or strengthened and who should do this.

Here are some examples of how to shape a vision through strategic planning. They refer to the illustrative fellowships that

Strategic Planning Guide
for _____ Church

I. IDENTIFYING SWOTS

CURRENT CHURCH RESOURCES		POSSIBLE NEEDS TO ADDRESS		POSSIBLE MAJOR GOALS
Strengths	Weaknesses	Opportunities	Threats	Satisfactions to Offer

II. EVALUATING ALTERNATIVES
Importance of outcomes

Feasibility with current resources

Fit with this congregation

III. CHOOSING A STRATEGY
Most reasonable now is:

To *Rely* on these Church Resources	To *Address* these Ministry Opportunities	To *Offer* these Satisfactions

IV. DEFERRING ACTION
New attention will be deferred on these ministry opportunities and goals:

V. PLANNING FOR IMPLEMENTATION
These programs should be developed:

These groups should be involved:

136

were introduced in chapter 7. Additional data is added to fill out the descriptions. After the headings are some entries that could go onto the Strategic Planning Guide for this church. Not all questions on the guide are answered in these examples.

St. Luke's

This is the symbolic fellowship with a membership of 500 and a weekly attendance of 200. The column entries after some discussion might look like this.

Strengths: worship well done, members loyal to congregation and denomination, good size, good building of adequate size, healthy finances, staff leadership, good support for pastor, two worship services.

Weaknesses: low attendance ratio, little visible sharing, little Bible study, no history of this function, few shared prayers, only one pastor, relatively few young people, small evangelism effort, little history of small groups.

Opportunities: city still growing, many young families in community, need for day care for the families in the community, need for more counseling, some members who want more fellowship, interest in small groups, need for a senior citizens group, an eager young adults group.

Threats: aging membership, insufficient staff.

Possible Satisfactions (goals): worship that is reassuring within an improved worship environment (organ), opportunity for relaxed, contemporary worship, filling affiliation needs through small-group sharing of Bible and prayer and through advanced discipleship groups, having more and better counseling, offering service to the community through day care.

Strategy: St. Luke's might adopt a strategy to continue the improved traditional worship service but to offer an alternative at an early service or on Saturday night, to make small-group interaction a priority, to look for staff personnel to develop fellowship life. Improvement of ministries through professional counseling and a day care center will be deferred.

Olive Fellowship

This is the group of young people who have been meeting in a home on Thursday evenings.

Strengths: attractive to young adults, a history of making decisions for themselves, Mrs. Jackson and her large house, a leadership core, participants who want to share, loyalty of many participants, no fixed expenses.

Weaknesses: losing its appeal, has not replaced leadership of two who left, current unstable leadership, no history of surviving transition.

Opportunities: reach more young adults, provide unique fellowship experience, leadership challenge for someone new, look to Mrs. Jackson for stability, look to Main Avenue Church for stability, legally incorporate to have better identity.

Threats: sudden decline if more conflict, eventual extinction, loss of appeal if no longer making own decisions.

Possible Satisfactions: having excitement of doing it on their own, making the group lively again, seeing the fellowship continue for many years, receiving the assistance of the ministry staff at Main Avenue Church, leaving behind an active fellowship for others.

Strategy: The leadership group had a hard time deciding whether independence or stability was more important. They agreed on a two-part strategy: to see how interested Main Avenue Church would be in including this fellowship in their ministry. If there is interest, to negotiate an arrangement in which they could maintain as much independence as possible. There was little interest in incorporation.

Christ Church

This is the church in the introduction to this chapter, with Bill Baumeister as pastor.

Strengths: growing membership, capable leadership, strong pastor, paid-for building, many ministries already established, good active fellowship life.

Weaknesses: limited growth potential in current building, lack of agreement on importance of growth.

Opportunities: develop other ministries within the current facility, some growth in current facility, almost unlimited growth if location is moved.

Threats: few apparent except limits for growth. Some members might leave if the location is changed and new debt incurred.

Possible Satisfactions: reaching more people with the Gospel, having the excitement of growth in numbers and facilities, new opportunities for ministry, the satisfaction of having all bills paid, having a new sanctuary, possibility of some growth without new debt.

Strategy: The majority of the committee wanted to relocate, but they worried that the membership would not be ready for this big step. They decided not to take action yet so they could have time to let the membership talk about and react to it. They hoped that the members would accept this vision for the future. They resolved to seek outside help to assess their vision of growth. They decided to develop a plan for involving the congregation in strategic planning.

Exploration Topic: Some Basics of Strategic Planning

Here are some principles for doing strategic planning in a local church. Leaders should have some preliminary ideas about a vision. These observations are for the bigger step of developing congregational input and commitment and finally a clarified, generally accepted vision. These principles cover the basics of strategic planning, the preparation that is advisable, and the four phases of the effort.

A. Emerging with a Shared Vision of Church Life

1. There should be an initial willingness to agree on preferences for the years ahead. These are the various dreams, intentions, and goals among the members of the congregation at large. Agreeing on preferences entails setting priorities.

2. There should be a readiness to promote good stewardship of church resources. The resources are the time, talent, and energy as well as the money of the members. Wastefulness happens when programs are started without success or when resources of the congregation are not fully utilized.

3. There should be a willingness and an ability to apply careful reasoning. This involves identifying causes and effects in church life. It also means looking at more than one alternative. Confidence about having chosen the best way to proceed is possible only when at least two other alternatives have been explored.

4. There should be a commitment to produce a written map to guide future efforts. This is the final written plan that presents

specific objectives and schedules as well as identification of responsibilities.

B. Assuring Necessary Conditions

1. A congregation should have a sense of purpose. It has to know why it exists to take seriously where it is going. Such purposes revolve around spiritual convictions. A church that has lost its sense of purpose needs to hear the Word of God and experience spiritual renewal. Preparation for that requires prayer, penitence, and solid spiritual leadership.

2. Members of a congregation should share a desire for change or improvement. There will be little response if most members feel that the church is fine the way it is. A church can raise its perspectives on reaching to greater heights by theological study combined with practical observation of what other churches are doing.

3. There should be an absence of serious conflict in the congregation. Planning can only pull people together when they want to work together. Time and careful, loving nurture may be needed to heal old wounds and restore enough sense of unity so that people can think constructively of the future.

4. The congregation should have an able leadership core. Planning usually generates many ideas for action and programs, but little implementation will happen in a congregation that has few members willing and able to accept leadership responsibility for change. In the absence of sufficient leadership, full-scale planning may have to be set aside temporarily in favor of planning toward the immediate objective of identifying and developing leaders.

5. The planning effort should be commissioned by the congregation.

C. Organizing the Planning Committee

1. Although the whole congregation should be interested in planning, responsibilities should be delegated to a planning group. A good size is 10 to 18 people. This limited number should facilitate an intensive level of discussion that stimulates insights and refines evaluations.

2. The committee should be regarded as a temporary task force that dissolves when the plan moves to implementation. Otherwise the regular organizational structure may not be ready to

implement what was planned by someone else or to think of good planning as their own responsibility. When it is done well, intensive planning should ordinarily not be needed for another five or ten years, or until circumstances change significantly.

3. The committee membership should be representative of the entire congregation and also present a mixture of characteristics. Among the participants should be people with

—knowledge of the congregation's programs, community, and history

—current positions of leadership in the congregation

—skills and analysis in communication

—ability to facilitate group decision making.

Members should be ready to commit themselves to about 30 hours of meeting time.

4. It is absolutely necessary that the pastor be involved with this committee. But someone else should chair it, preferably an aggressive, experienced leader. When the pastor serves as chairperson, there is a risk that the resulting plan will be received by the congregation as a statement of the pastor's intentions rather than their own. The committee may want to divide its work among several subcommittees to concentrate on the study areas they have defined.

5. The right amount of time to allow for planning is enough to be thorough but not so much that participants get bored or lose sight of completion. There should be more than one meeting and just a little less than a full annual church-year cycle.

D. Establishing Study Areas

Planners will mostly see what they are prepared to see, and they can easily be overwhelmed when they lack guidelines. Before beginning assignments, it is important to divide church life into major areas that members can concentrate on.

Basic divisions would be internal growth, external growth, and supportive operations. Many churches recognize five major functions, which could be grouped as reaching inward (worship and nurture), reaching outward (service and witnessing), and support. Understood as defined here, there would be no separate function of fellowship; all of church life is the fellowship.

E. Four Planning Phases

Assuming that the previously discussed preparation has been done, the planning process can be separated into four important phases.

Phase One: Assessing Needs and Resources. Planning begins with something like a SWOTS analysis of the congregation in the various study areas that were established at the outset. The sub-committees could work just with what is in their heads and hearts, or they could engage in extensive interviewing, surveying, and data gathering. But information is not an end in itself, and the group must avoid letting the desire for more information block the rest of the planning.

Phase Two: Evaluating Desired Outcomes. The SWOTS analysis leads naturally into the formulation of *goals* (satisfactions). These can be regarded as snapshots of what the congregation would look like when the needs are met. Possible outcomes should be narrowed down to a manageable number of important or vital outcomes. Several alternatives should be identified for each so that the group can select the best.

Phase Three: Selecting Task Steps. Planning does not mean doing the actual work. But the action steps necessary to achieve the outcome should be identified. The outline of task steps should be specific enough to guide those who will follow them but general enough to leave room for creativity and initiative. This phase involves more than coming up with good ideas for others to do. The constant question should be whether the church has reasonably sufficient resources to carry out the proposed plan.

Phase Four: Providing for Implementation. The reward for the planning effort is seeing dozens and hundreds of church members doing things they might not have tried otherwise. The objective for the final phase is getting all the potential doers willing and excited to commit their resources to new directions. If this objective is poorly met, the planners will leave little more than a report that is soon forgotten. Yet having a clearly written report is critical. Also crucial is leaving opportunities for other church leaders to test the plan before they are asked to endorse it. When the plan is formally recognized and accepted by the congregation, a celebration of intentions is important.

Chapter 9 _____

Getting Fellow Workers into Place

Pastor Bill Baumeister of Christ Church was reflecting as he planned his week. He was mulling over some ideas he had gained in recent reading and discussions. Many of the images that came to mind seemed helpful. But he was not sure what to do about them.

I like the architect image, he thought. I'm a good carpenter minister, and I have been doing a lot of contracting in this church. But I always thought there was more to leadership than just keeping things going. The challenge of shaping this church's vision is exciting.

We could use more lively stones here, he continued. But I'm glad we have as many as we do, and I feel confident that we can do better at helping passives become livelies, especially through more small-group activity. I can think of at least four more potential cornerstones, and I am looking forward to figuring out how to turn them loose. I just hope we can keep life rewarding for all the workers here, especially those who take leadership.

Having a full-bodied fellowship here at Christ Church is not out of the question, he thought with a smile. Not only are we gaining in attendance, but overall activity seems up, and I can think of a lot of members who serve for the best of reasons. But maybe this is just a temporary upswing after all the troubles of the past. I don't think we are ready to be serious about a new building and location until we do more planning. I'm curious whether that SWOTS stuff would help.

Dare I use marketing images with our leaders? Bill wondered. Turning seekers into finders makes a lot of sense, and we can certainly do better packaging. But I am not sure how far we want to go with talk about exchanges. Transformational leadership is what we need. Can I really do that? Will God bless my efforts?

It's time to get really practical. Where should we start?

Starting with the Right Image

Even after selecting a starting point for new leadership efforts, few things are more practical than a good image to guide discovery of the right actions.

One of the best images can be uncovered in the familiar first part of Eph. 4:12: "to prepare God's people for works of service." This phrase is the apostle Paul's most direct, all-encompassing statement of what church leaders are supposed to do. Its present significance lies in the bridge it carefully builds between the key concepts of this discussion of church leadership. Directly before it is the list of God-given leaders: apostles, prophets, evangelists, pastors and teachers. After it comes the object of their intent: building fellowship in the body of Christ. (See chapter 2 for this translation of "so that the body of Christ may be built up," as the NIV puts it.) The middle phrase presents the primary action the church leaders are to take. But the image remains blurred in most translations. Try this one: God gave church leaders *to get fellow members into place for the work of service* to build fellowship in the body of Christ. Key to the image is the action of aligning people, adapting, adjusting, or fitting them together—getting them into place.

The RSV term "equipping" is crisper than "preparing" (NIV), but both lack a dimension reflected in the King James "perfecting." And all three lack yet another dimension of the Greek *katartismos*, which Paul used to describe what the leaders are to do. Of the seven other New Testament occurrences of this word, the most frequent translation is "to restore," conveying a sense of a standard toward which a believer is to be moved; "perfecting" picks up this thrust (cf. 2 Cor. 13:11; Gal. 6:1; and 1 Peter 5:10). Three others stress action aimed at not one but several parts—fitting, adjusting, or uniting them together (cf. Rom. 9:22; 1 Cor. 1:10; and Heb. 11:3). Thus the overall sense can be action that moves parts of a whole toward alignment with each other—getting them into place.

In Eph 4:12 the measure that tells whether the parts are suitably in place is the work of service that builds fellowship. If the work does not sufficiently build fellowship, the leaders' task is to keep trying to get the members better fitted together with each other so that their service can more effectively build. And of course, according to verse 13, fellowship building is not sufficiently done until *all* arrive at unity of faith and knowledge, become complete persons, and reach the heights of the fullness of Christ.

A word study like this seems heavy for a chapter introduction, but the word and its image are crucial for what follows. Also important is the word—and image—in Eph 4:12 that identifies those who are to be aligned with each other. "The saints" is the literal translation, softened in the NIV to "God's people." In Paul's usage, the saints are not an abstract category for all who believe. He repeatedly uses it as a special affectionate term to address the members of the local congregation to which he is writing, and he particularly associates it with Christians who are sharing love with one another, demonstrated in practical service.[1] In this sense of the sanctified who are committed to their fellowship, the saints are rendered here as "fellow members."

It is but a short step to define the task as "getting fellow workers into place"—a summary of "getting fellow members into place for the work of service."

Fellowship building is much too great a task for just one leader—pastoral or other—to even think about taking on alone. Fitting workers into a specific congregation is much too complicated for any one leader at the outset even to pretend to know exactly how it should look.

The most appropriate and easiest starting point is to gather the company of fellow workers who will help shape the vision and give legs and leadership to the effort. This is also the most natural starting point theologically, for what is built should be the expression of the whole fellowship, not just of the pastor. Theoretically, all members of the fellowship are the base point, but practically speaking, an architecturally inclined pastor will do better to concentrate first on the lively stones and cornerstones who are available to do most of the early work. And it is more practical still to concentrate on the lively stones and potential cornerstones who are the recognized leaders.

Thus, getting leader/workers into place is the most advisable immediate starting point. Many of these, in turn, can carry on

---

[1] Cf. G. W. Lampe, *Interpreter's Dictionary of the Bible* (Abingdon, 1962), 4:164–165, s.v. "the saints"; also Wayne A. Meeks, *The First Urban Christians* (Yale, 1983), p. 85.

as contractors to get other workers into place and widen the worker network.

Here are some more-or-less specific steps and images that can guide this phase of leadership:

1. *Look for both parts and plants.* The trick is to know when to look for which.

2. *Provide both support and structure.* Again, the trick is to know when to provide which and where.

3. *Resolve to compensate and protect the workers.* This is a fundamental task of good personnel management.

4. *Aim to develop a spiritual gifts administration program.* This is a systematic way to discover and guide what each member can contribute.

5. *Give all a steady diet of strong spiritual feeding.*

For the spiritual leader, the constant task is to challenge and comfort with God's Word.

1. Look for Parts and Plants

It is surprising how much management understanding and advice can be summarized under two images: a machine and a living organism. They form the bases for the two best established approaches toward understanding and developing organization— the structural and the human resources approaches, as discussed in most texts on management or organizational behavior.[2] Management is usually defined as accomplishing objectives through others. The two images suggest alternate and complementary ways of approaching those who are to be involved in a managed effort. The challenge is to learn when to think which way.

The participants can be approached as *parts* for assembly into a machine. Accordingly, to accomplish certain objectives, there is an idealized concept of the specialized contributions that each worker will make and of preferred relationships between workers as they do their assigned tasks. The basic management emphasis is on designing structure in the abstract, much as an engineer designs an engine with interacting parts. The leader's task is to find people to fit into the predetermined structure, to describe exactly what they are supposed to do, and to keep them interacting and performing according to these expectations. With

---

[2] Cf. Lee G. Bolman and Terrence E. Deal, *Modern Approaches to Understanding and Managing Organizations* (Jossey Bass, 1984).

this mind-set toward pursuing an improved joint effort, leaders look for parts to be added to or refined within the machine.

Alternately, participants can be approached as *plants* to be grown in a garden. The garden must be cultivated to bring out the full potential of all the various seedlings or full-grown bushes. With a general purpose like beauty or fruitfulness, specific purposes may shift as the composition or stage of development of the garden shifts. The relationships between plants may also change as they grow at various rates. The leader's main task is to recognize the plants that are present and to cultivate them. Improvement comes by adding new plants and carefully placing all so that the potential of each is most fully realized.

By itself, neither of these basic images sufficiently describes how most organizations are effectively managed. Each produces powerful insights and guidance, or it would not persist. Each has distinct limits, or the other would not persist. Approaching organization as a machine, with an emphasis on structure, permits clear and efficient design for the interaction of workers. But it does not provide much help for dealing with how real human participants often actually act, especially when they do not care much about their assigned part. Approaching organization as an organism, with emphasis on adaptation to participants' needs and interests, permits creative development and effective use of human potential. But it is often weak in bringing the various efforts together into a well-coordinated, long-lasting, and widely shared response to demands of the marketplace or external environment, especially when effectiveness depends on efficiency.

When to think which way is one of the primary skills to be learned in becoming a better manager. This amounts to learning the contingencies. To summarize a vast amount of research and corporate experience, looking for plants to cultivate in a garden makes sense when tasks cannot be clearly defined and individual creativity and commitment is important for progress in a department or organization, especially when overall coordination is not important. Looking for parts to assemble in an already determined structure makes sense when there is confidence that the tasks and means for achieving them are well defined and when an average degree of personal commitment is sufficient for accomplishing the purposes. To assure greater stability and to lessen demands on leaders, organizations typically settle into machinelike thinking, with supplementary efforts at cultivating plants and gardens.

How These Images Apply to Churches

These images are hardly new concepts; they are almost explicit in Biblical thinking about the church. Paul describes his leader relationship to church members: "For we [Apollos and Paul] are God's fellow workers; you [the Corinthian fellowship members] are God's field, God's building" (1 Cor 3:9).

Looking at the Corinthian church as a field or garden, Paul sees himself planting the seed and Apollos watering it, although clearly God is the one who gives the growth (v. 6). Apollos and Paul were spiritual leaders, to be sure: "Only servants, through whom you came to believe" (v. 5). They recognized the diverse contributions that each fellowship member brought "as the Lord has assigned to each his task" (v. 5). The objective is for the garden to grow (vv. 7–8).

Looking at these Christians as a building or house (or God's temple in which the Spirit lives, v. 16), Paul sees the leadership task as carefully putting the right pieces together on the right foundation (vv. 11–13). In the text that forms the basis for the architectural theme, he also sees himself as the expert, guiding other builders who came later (v. 10). Different parts can go into the house: gold, silver, costly stones, wood, hay, or straw (v. 12). The objective is that the house be durable and survive (vv. 13–14).

There is no reason to conclude that Paul considered one image to be better than the other. He could think both ways. He did put garden and house in stunning juxtaposition (v. 9). In other applications of his leadership viewpoint, he clearly approached the church as an organism; this is the "body of Christ" image that he used repeatedly. But with the same congregations he repeatedly used the image of a building; building a house is the core image of the concept of fellowship building that is developed here.

Were we to pursue how Paul might have seen a relationship between the integrating images of an organism and of a building, we could find hints a few verses after his magnificent statement of leader purpose and focus in Eph. 4. In verses 15–16 Paul envisions that we Christians will all grow up into Christ the Head, from whom the whole body, held together by every supporting ligament, "grows and builds itself up in love." The Greek text is complicated. A more literal and accurate translation is that the body held together by its ligaments "produces growth of the body for its fellowship building in love." Growth appears to be a contribution to building. This is also the order in which Paul put the garden and the building in 1 Cor. 3.

Advice to Church Builders/Leaders

1. *Start new efforts by looking for plants.* To begin a new building emphasis in church leadership, look first for plants. These are members who are ready for themselves and the church to grow into something different. They will most likely catch and shape a vision for mission easily and model the momentum that can bring others along. Be prepared to find key potential builders in various corners of the fellowship, whether or not they are in the formal church organization. Recognize them as gifts of the Spirit. Get them planted where they can start working, whether or not that is in a formal position. Cultivate them carefully.

2. *Recognize and respect the parts already in place.* All but a brand-new congregation will have an established organization with formal leaders already in place. Most visible church leaders will be in a formal position. Know them well. Respect them; they have accepted responsibility to keep the processes of routine church life going, often with outstanding dedication. Many may be promising plants ready to grow in new ways. Among all the parts, expect different reactions to new leader initiatives; some may have other visions, and others may be afraid of any vision. Try to work with and through them as much as possible, and always keep them informed. But do not be discouraged when they resist. Keep cultivating the growing plants. Let them grow into the formal organization and shape it.

3. *Don't rush to rewrite the constitution.* This is an initial impulse of many pastors and church leaders frustrated with their church organization. But to fashion a new written document will only substitute one ineffective abstract design for another if the fellowship is not already moved by a vision of interacting in different ways. This design most likely will focus on the governance structure. The ministry structure is more important at early stages of new church building effort, and it can remain rather informal. Much can be accomplished without the need for formal governance votes. Keep cultivating the growing plants. The need for formalized change will become apparent over time.

4. *Assemble a tighter structure as the vision and tasks become clearer.* Much of an improved structure of working relationships can precede change in the constitutional arrangements. As the momentum for new fellowship building grows, the demand for more supportive and efficient organization will increase. As the need for improvement grows, don't be afraid to involve others in thinking about a better design of positions and responsibilities. When the better organization is apparent, be ready to find and fit the necessary parts together. Machinelike structures have their place, although few retain their vitality for long periods.

5. *Approach full-time staff as parts as well as plants.* Full-time paid staff members are special believers who usually need to keep growing to retain their commitment and vision for their work. They are also special resources of a fellowship, usually representing their largest financial investment. Such staff people will be most likely to contribute best to overall fellowship building when the expectations for their contributions are clearly defined and their efforts are carefully coordinated. Assemble a staff carefully, and be ready to keep their efforts aligned with a building design that shows the place where their part best fits.

2. Provide Both Support and Structure

Leadership has slightly different reference points among those who talk and teach it. One is the grand scale of providing vision and direction for a relatively large number of people, such as a whole congregation. This is the understanding usually heard among those addressing nonprofit organizations, such as government (James Burnes and his transformational leadership) or education (Lee Bolman and Terrence Deal with their political and symbolic approaches). Such is the present general understanding of church leadership, especially in the concept of the architect.

A much more limited reference point is the leadership exercised through direct personal interaction with those who are being led. This is the more common meaning in business management, discussed as supervision. Many of the insights come from study of small-group leadership.

For pastors, the task of getting fellowship workers into place must include personal interaction with them one by one or in small work groups. "Supervision" may be a somewhat alien notion when applied to the collaboration of pastor and people (although it should not be within a paid staff relationship). Nevertheless, the leadership practiced by supervisors can provide sound, practical guidance to help a pastor and others become better leaders of fellowship building.

A huge amount of research has gone into discovering why some supervisory leaders are more effective than others. Two relatively blind alleys are that certain traits distinguish effective leaders and that there is one best way of leading. The mainstream of understanding and advice has focused on distinguishing two dimensions of leader behavior for improved insight and practice. Although various terms are used, the images of providing structure and offering support (or consideration) capture much of what should be done. The first is an application of the larger structural (machine) approach and the second of the human resource (organism) approach to organization and management.

Leading others through personal interaction often amounts to providing *support* for their efforts. This can be done in dozens of ways. In working with others, leaders would do well to concentrate on:

1. *developing feelings of approval*, so that the others actually feel that they and their contributions are important and appreciated. This is often done by showing interest in what they are doing, listening to their difficulties, giving praise where justified, and helping overcome mistakes where necessary.

2. *being interested in them individually*, so that they feel appreciated for who they are as well as what they do. This can be done by having frequent contact with them, listening to their personal problems, showing an interest in their families, and hearing their aspirations.

3. *assuring fair treatment* so they will not feel exploited. What is important is not so much the leader's perception but the group's perception of fairness; all need to feel confident that others in the same situation would be treated the same way.

Effective leadership often also calls for behavior that provides *structure* for the efforts of others. Among many ways to do that would be these basic actions:

1. *setting objectives* so that those in the work group do not waste their efforts in confusion about what to do. Structure of this sort contributes to clarifying what the outcome should look like and what standards it should meet.

2. *guiding work efforts* so that people know not only what to do but also how to accomplish their tasks. This can be done

by providing, where necessary, detailed instruction, by offering prior training, or by being available for questions.

3. *providing technical assistance* so they have the means to get the job done well and easily. Providing information can often be more important than tools or materials.[3]

Variations on support and structure are almost endless. Church work would have its own adaptations, especially where workers are involved in basic functions of a church's life. The way a leader combines both emphases amounts to leadership style. Each leader will have a characteristic style. The most effective leaders are able to vary their style as needed.

One of the most important skills for leadership at the interpersonal level is knowing when to emphasize which type of leadership behavior. Offering both support and structure is usually important at some time or another, but one is likely to be more important than the other under certain circumstances. What are those circumstances? Management researchers talk about them as contingencies—factors on which something depends.

The answer lies in figuring out what the workers need, and this often gets down to what each individual needs. How to lead depends on what the worker and workers will find helpful for continuing and improving their performance. "Situational leadership" is a term used to describe this approach.

Paul Hersey and Ken Blanchard offer a framework for practicing situational leadership that has easy and interesting application to churches.[4] They focus on supportive (relationship) behavior and directive (structuring) behavior. The key contingency—that on which the right mix of leader behavior depends—is the maturity level of the followers. This refers not to general personal maturity (or spiritual maturity, we might say in churches) but to task maturity—the ability and willingness to take responsibility for directing their own behavior toward performing the tasks at hand. To complicate matters, one individual may have high maturity for one task (like performing office routines) but low maturity for another (like planning a learning session for children).

---

[3] These summaries of support and structural leadership behavior are based on George Stauss and Leonard R. Sayles, *Personnel: The Human Problem of Management.* 4th ed. (Prentice Hall, 1980).

[4] Paul Hersey and Ken Blanchard, *Management of Organizational Behavior: Utilizing Human Resources.* 4th ed. (Prentice Hall, 1982), pp. 149–72.

Hersey and Blanchard set forth this diagram to summarize their advice to leaders:

STYLE OF LEADER

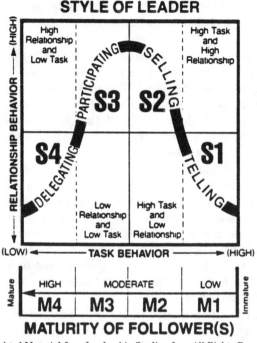

Copyrighted Material from Leadership Studies, Inc. All Rights Reserved. Used by Permission.

There are four possible combinations of the two basic behaviors: high on both, low on both, high on one and low on the other, and vice versa. These are the four cells of the large box and the four basic styles. For simplicity, Hersey and Blanchard call them Telling (Style 1), Selling (Style 2), Participating (Style 3), and Delegating (Style 4). They further distinguish four relative maturity levels—M1 (low) to M4 (high).

Their advice for leading others with little preparation or willingness for the job is to be task- and structure-directed in leadership behavior—Telling. An example is the supervisory style for first-job teenagers (M1) in a McDonalds.

Adding strong supportive, relationship behavior to high task direction (Selling) becomes important for followers at the next level of maturity (M2). They generally are willing to give the necessary effort but do not know how. They need task direction and also reinforcement for their enthusiasm. One popular view is that leader behavior should strive to be high support and high task (S2) all the time, but for M1 and M4 followers, high leader support is likely to be wasteful and confusing, and for M3 followers high task behavior is likely to be redundant and even resented.

The next level of task maturity (M3) describes followers who know how to do the job but may lack confidence or may even be unwilling to make the effort. Directive, task-structuring leadership behavior is no longer so important. Supportive, nondirective behavior, with the leader facilitating shared decision making, has the highest probability of effectiveness in this situation. This is the Participating (S3) style.

Finally, followers who have high task maturity (M4) need little leadership at all. Continued discussion of the task and showing interest is important, but these behaviors can remain at a low level. An example is the relation of a hospital administrator to physicians on the medical staff. The doctors know much more about their healing tasks than the administrator, and they typically look to each other for encouragement, not to someone outside their profession. The administrator can do well with a Delegating (S4) style.

How could this Hersey/Blanchard model, which can be considerably expanded, apply to pastors and churches? It is useful in proportion to how well it can guide church leadership effort to get workers into place effectively for fellowship building.

The main lesson is not to underestimate the variance in the maturity of the followers. The corollary lesson is to be ready to exercise a continually changing variety of leadership styles. What such differences might look like for ministers, both in theological emphases and pastoral practice, is explored by David S. Luecke and Samuel Southard in *Pastoral Administration: Integrating Ministry and Management*,[5] which is organized around support and structure themes.

Here are some generalizations: In recent decades many pastors have reacted strongly against the directive (Telling) style of earlier generations of pastors as too authoritarian. A rising gen-

---

[5] Cf. David S. Luecke and Samuel Southard, *Pastoral Administration: Integrating Ministry and Management* (Word Publishing, 1986), for further discussion of developing a pastor's leadership style, especially chapter 1.

eral educational level of church members would make such a shift reasonable. But there are still many segments of society where believers come with limited maturity for self-direction in church activity, especially for more abstract tasks like planning and developing. Need for the high leadership task orientations of Telling and Selling styles may be greater than many pastors are ready to recognize. This may also be true within a specific congregation, where some highly visible members may display higher maturity, but many potential workers remain almost immobilized without clear directions.

Many pastors instinctively gravitate toward the fourth style of leader behavior—Delegating. It is certainly the least demanding in time and effort, for neither high relationship nor high task leader behavior is important. But the circumstances in which such delegating is effective are quite narrow and assume the most of others. In many cases, pastors who prefer this approach are simply abrogating personal leadership. All other things being equal (and assuming a socially middle- to upper-class congregation), the potential fellowship builders to be encountered today will usually expect a fairly high level of supportive relationships to sustain their participation. Thus the selling and participating leadership styles are likely to be the most effective approaches for pastors to take, with task-directive emphases being the leadership behavior to modify according to need.

Advice to Church Leaders/Builders on Leader Style

1. *Look first for what the followers need.* The temptation is to look first toward the kind of interpersonal leadership behavior a pastor or other leader wants to provide. There may even be a theological understanding behind this preference. But the real question is the task maturity of each individual and each group of followers.

2. *Resolve to provide well for the full range of follower task-related needs.* Few leaders personally have the ability to do this in interpersonal leadership, even if they had the time. Starting with the followers, however, will bring greater readiness to search for other means to provide leadership initiatives most appropriate for each worker.

3. *Recognize your own dominant leadership style.* Each

leader is usually most comfortable with one emphasis in style, and few can move equally well between the alternatives. This is a matter of recognizing strengths and weaknesses. It is important to work from strengths for both effectiveness and personal satisfaction.

4. *Appreciate leaders whose style is different.* They can be frustrating to work with. But leaders who approach others with a different style can provide valuable complementary leadership and move work effort to higher levels of performance.

5. *Team up.* There are many important reasons to concentrate on developing a team of fellow leaders. Challenging and complementing each other in leadership style is a basic one.

3. Resolve to Compensate and Protect

A personnel director looking at the function of getting workers into place would have some pretty clear ideas about what needs to be done. In addition to being quite conversant with the issues raised so far in this chapter, the director would want to know more about how individuals are selected and placed for their contribution. A personnel director would especially want to see provisions made for training, compensating, and protecting workers.

Leave selection and placement for the next section of this chapter. Questions of training are familiar in churches, but compensation and protection are not thought about much, especially for workers other than paid staff.

Consider the leadership function of getting and keeping workers best placed for fellowship building from the viewpoint of assuring that they have a good experience and trying to avoid bad things that might happen to them.

Providing for a rewarding experience is the essence of compensation. Paying dollars is but one way, and a relatively easy one. Practical church leaders mostly must look for other ways, and these other ways can potentially be more significant. People are likely to react to their work as a positive experience when it gives them recognition and appreciation, a sense of responsibility, feelings of achievement, or opportunities for growth. Churches and their leaders can resolve to keep looking for opportunities to give these forms of compensation. Not doing so is one of the most common failures in administering church work. Members should certainly contribute their time and effort out of transformed allegiance to Christ and His body. But such good intentions are best buttressed with ongoing compensation in human terms.

Proper preparation for a task is one of the best provisions for satisfaction in doing it. Lack of attention to training and development is another common weakness in administering church work. Perhaps one reason is lack of concern for compensation.

If accentuating the positive is not sufficient reason for careful preparation and placement, avoiding negatives may be more persuasive. This forms the leader's responsibility to protect the worker and those affected by his or her work. Individual or group failure is a hard burden for a fellowship to carry. Judging from his letters, Paul spent considerable time worrying about failure in various churches and showing ways to avoid or overcome it.

Getting members into the right place and having them well prepared for their work is one of the best protections that can be given them as well as the fellowship.

4. Aim for a Spiritual Gifts Administration Program

In the introduction to this chapter, Pastor Bill Baumeister was wondering how to get started with new efforts. Many of the images had triggered ideas for new possibilities. Pastor Bill had now served this congregation for several years and was committed to several program efforts he had stimulated. Should he try to launch a new fellowship-building program? What would it be? Why didn't someone just give him the program he needed?

The urge to initiate a program is strong in most pastors who want to exert church leadership—for good reason. As developed in chapter 4, programming is the most direct administrative process of "pulling" followers into action. Looking for parts and plants, providing support and structure, and resolving to compensate and protect may be necessary to get the workers into place. But what are they to do? How do we get to some action?

Try this: The program that offers the most promise to pull into focused interaction a broad and fresh mixture of workers and their contributions is one that concentrates on discovering and challenging the spiritual gifts present in a congregation. Every fellowship member has something to contribute. Find it and help that member put it to use for the common good. Doing so systematically is the basis for an exciting and practical program that is likely to pull all sorts of other administrative program development behind it.

The Biblical base of spiritual gifts administration was highlighted in chapter 4. In 1 Cor. 12:4–7 Paul celebrates the diversity of gifts, services, and workings given by the same God and Spirit, and he declares: "Now to each one the manifestation of the Spirit is given for the common good." Although present in individual members, these are gifts to the whole congregation. In Rom. 12:6–8, Paul again declares that the members have different gifts according to God's grace. Now let each, he says, get on with exercising that gift, whatever it might be, for the body, and he offers examples. Peter states: "Each one should use whatever gift he has received to serve others" and adds the charge: "faithfully administering God's grace in its various forms" (1 Peter 4:10). A congregation's administration of what members moved by the Spirit are ready to offer can be done more faithfully when it is done systematically through a well-considered and implemented program. Specifics will vary because in God's grace the leaders will differ in the specific gifts they bring to the task. But such a program has to revolve around carefully discovering the many gifts present among fellowship members. This is where a personnel director would start. Gifts inventory questionnaires are available for that purpose or can be developed. But no program would go far without also carefully planning for and providing opportunities to exercise those contributions. This in turn necessitates identifying leaders who, in effect, can serve as contractors to match workers to needs according to broad categories of congregational interaction such as programs within worship, nurture, witnessing, and service areas. Some sort of overall administration like this goes on in most congregations, but usually rather informally. Organizing this leadership effort formally and deliberately can be a new frontier in church work. Extending it from the leaders to every member would be an unusual accomplishment.

Recall the exchange dynamics basic to fellowship sharing, as presented in chapter 5. Note the direction such a gifts administration program takes for increasing the exchange. It emphasizes the flow of activity from the individual to the fellowship. The opposite flow of the fellowship offering to the individual has to remain basic to developing specific conventional programs like those found in education and service. But that flow draws on energy and resources without necessarily replenishing them. Developing all the gifts provides momentum for the giving, not just the receiving. "Find a need and fill it" will always be basic to bringing people into the fellowship and increasing their participation. "Find the gifts and put them to work" is the complementary motto. It has more potential for building an existing fellowship to new levels of sharing.

A spiritual gifts administration program cannot just be announced and launched within a month or so. The key word in this plan of action is to "aim" for such an effort. Simply giving everyone a spiritual gifts inventory and hoping for more activity is a prescription for major disappointment, as countless pastors have discovered. A framework for guiding these contributions must first take shape. But even more important, for this approach to work the members really must be "moved by the Spirit" to see their participation in new ways. Preparation for such movement needs to be done by the last practical step to be mentioned here.

5. Give Steady Spiritual Feeding

In church life, nothing is more practical than the Gospel at work changing lives. To build fellowship, a pastor will need to be a leader of organization and programs. But above all, a pastor is the leader of the spiritual means by which God calls and moves His followers.

Through His Word and sacraments, God continually comforts those who turn to Him. Through solid, Biblical preaching and teaching, the spiritual leader of a congregation conveys that comfort in words and strives to see it implemented in deeds. Through His Word and sacraments God also gives His people strength to reach new and higher levels of response beyond comfort—to build the body of Christ and to reach for the heights of the fullness of Christ in doing so. Continually delivering those life-giving means of grace with full force and compelling necessity is the leadership contribution the pastor is specially called and uniquely qualified to make.

When looking for where to start fresh fellowship building effort in a congregation, the best place is with this necessary basic task. Out of steady Biblical, spiritual feeding come the seeds of new church vision and energy. By themselves, new conceptual images and organizational techniques may bring some change here and there. But new bursts of exciting building will not occur without the sustaining and nourishing power of the Holy Spirit at work in the fellowship through the means of grace. Leading in a church has many dimensions. Yet there is no substitute for basic spiritual feeding.

Chapter 10 _____

Conclusion: Be Leaders
in a Partnership of Joy

Church leaders are *God's gift to His church* (Eph. 4:11; Rom. 12:8; 1 Cor. 12:28). If you are a church leader, your work is crucial. The unavoidable need for good leaders is apparent in any organized effort in society, as witnessed by the decline that occurs when good leadership is absent. God saw the need from the beginnings of His people. You are to be part of the answer today.

Church leaders are called for *many different roles and contributions*. This is the point of the emphasis on diversity in the Biblical passages dealing with the work of the one Spirit in 1 Cor. 12, Rom. 12, and Eph. 4. If you are a pastoral leader, you will need the help of many colleagues in your church. If you are an elder, deacon, trustee, or chairperson, don't let anyone think that you are "just" a lay leader; your contribution is important wherever you are called and gifted to make it.

Church leadership should be *done with passion*. This is Paul's message to Timothy (2 Tim. 1:5, 7). The necessary cause for enthusiasm for the job is in sincerely holding the faith of the church. "For this reason I remind you to fan into flame the gift of God, which is in you through the laying on of my hands. For God did not give us a spirit of timidity, but a spirit of power, of love and of self-discipline" (vv. 6–7). The laying on of hands is especially done for pastors and their gift. In a figurative sense this is what happens whenever a congregation recognizes someone as a leader by election or appointment. Don't be timid. Get excited about your contribution.

Church leaders should *recognize high standards*. It is Paul's expectation that churches will be led to attain "the whole measure of the fullness of Christ"—to excel (Eph. 4:13). As Paul reminds fellow builders who follow him, they can build "using gold, silver, costly stones, wood, hay or straw" and their work "will be shown for what it is" (1 Cor. 3:12, 13). Examples of church leaders who

161

usually settle for the easiest course of action can be readily found. Don't be one of those, grasping for whatever solution is at hand, whether it be like cheap hay or straw. Insist that you and your colleagues go for the gold. Pursue excellence for your church.

Church leaders should *be ready for the frustrations* of dealing with church realities that can be far from the ideal. There is a little of the Corinthian congregation in most churches: "quarreling, jealousy, outbursts of anger, factions, slander, gossip, arrogance and disorder" (2 Cor. 12:20). Remember that "we have this treasure in jars of clay to show that this all-surpassing power is from God and not from us" (4:7).

Church leadership can be *personally risky*. These risks probably will not be as dramatic as they were for leaders in the early church who were persecuted by those outside the church: imprisonment (Peter and Paul), hunger, thirst, brutal treatment (1 Cor. 4:11), and martyrdom—although these reactions can be found today in other parts of the world. But there will be risks in relation to those already in the church. They may want to choose sides (3:3–4). Some will oppose new ideas by focusing on the persons of those who advance them (16:9). Many will negatively judge leadership efforts prematurely (4:5). Even church people cannot refrain from gossip and petty criticism about their leaders (9:3–14). They may be contemptuous of physical appearance or speech (2 Cor. 10:10). Like Paul, be prepared to discover that people in the church may not see you as you want to be seen (12:20). If you want to be an effective leader, recognize that the work will not always be pleasant. This is a basic reason why a partnership of joy is so important.

Church leaders should even *be prepared for times of despondency* when they come close to losing hope and want to give up. Paul knew the feeling: "We are hard pressed on every side, but not crushed; perplexed, but not in despair; persecuted, but not abandoned; struck down, but not destroyed" (4:9–10). Hope returns as we remember the resurrection, by which the life of Jesus can be revealed in us. "Death [may be] at work in us, but life is at work in you [church members]" (v. 12). Even—or especially—in this setting Paul invites us to find joy, as we shall see.

Church leadership can be *stressful hard work*, especially if it is not shared with other leaders. This is the lesson that leader Moses had to learn among God's Old Testament people. His father-in-law, Jethro, saw what was happening. "You and these people who come to you will only wear yourselves out. The work is too heavy for you; you cannot handle it alone" (Ex. 18:18). Help would come by recognizing others as leadership colleagues. Jethro even saw that as a command of God: "That will make your load lighter, because they will share it with you. If you do this and God so commands, you will be able to stand the strain, and all these people will go home satisfied" (vv. 22–23). This sharing is basic to the partnership that Paul holds out as the way church leadership should be at its best. To that we now turn.

The Model Partnership of Joy[1] *at Philippi*

Yes, church leaders of today accept a responsibility that can be heavy and trying, albeit critical. The frequent unpleasant realities make it all the more important to keep the joyful side of church leadership in perspective. Without the carefully cultivated joy, leadership can too easily become something to withdraw from and hope someone else will pick up.

Paul and the leaders of the church at Philippi have much to teach present-day church leaders, pastoral and lay. After summarizing the good thing they had going, we will look at some specific pointers, like keeping the partnership spiritually based, setting sights high, exercising partnership by encouraging and comforting each other, working hard to settle disagreements, and showing special care for each other.

Paul specifically addressed the leaders of only one church among all those to which he wrote. He usually addressed all the believers. Only to the Philippians did he write: "To all the saints in Christ Jesus . . . together with the overseers and deacons" (Phil. 1:1). Although all the saints come first, he leaves the impression that he is really talking to the leaders. This is the sense conveyed in J. B. Phillips' version: "to the bishops, deacons, and all true Christians at Philippi."

The letter to the Philippians is the source of many well-memorized, oft-quoted passages beloved over the ages. These are often interpreted as applying to Christians individually, as they certainly can be. But the "you" that is used so often is plural, not singular. And the second person plural brings a slightly dif-

---

[1] The concept of a partnership of joy was suggested by a chapter title in Jonathan F. Grothe's *Reclaiming Patterns of Pastoral Ministry*, Concordia; 1988.

ferent flavor when focused specifically on the leaders—the bishops and deacons. Paul's exhortations, remembrances, and comments of care will be interpreted here according to that specific reference; he will be viewed as talking to his fellow leaders. Accordingly, he is seen as modeling an exchange that can take place between the pastor and other leaders of a congregation today.

Significantly, the Greek word for fellowship, *koinōnia*, shows up six times in this letter, which is more often per chapter than in any other New Testament writing. Sometimes it refers to the vertical relationship with God. Sometimes it relates to horizontal relationships of sharing between believers in general. And sometimes it can be interpreted as a special sharing between Paul and the Philippians, especially their leaders. This latter sense will be rendered here as "partnership." Paul felt an unusually close partnership with the Philippian leaders. We can see it as a special partnership within the larger fellowship.

It was a partnership of joy. The words for joy show up in this short letter more often than in any other. Over and over Paul urges the people to rejoice; they can be glad. Paul remembers many things they did for his joy, and he is cheered. He purposefully does things for their joy. Their joy will overflow because of him (1:26). They are his joy and crown (4:1). "I am glad and rejoice with all of you. So you too should be glad and rejoice with me" (2:17–18).

The familiarity of the words can cause us to miss their significance for those responsible for a congregation. These leaders really enjoyed each other with a joy that put everything else into a good and satisfying perspective.

How did Paul and the Philippian leaders develop this great working relationship? How were they keeping it up?

How can a pastor and the other leaders of a church arrive at such a supportive, enjoyable relationship today? What should they do to keep it going? Let Paul show the way.

1. Keep the partnership spiritually based.
a. Expect your joy to come from the Lord.
(Pastor) "I rejoice greatly *in the Lord* when you show concern" (4:10).
(Leaders) "For the rest, colleagues, rejoice *in the Lord*" (3:1). "Rejoice *in the Lord* always. I will say it again: Rejoice" (4:4).

Happiness, fulfillment, or joy can be found in many aspects of leadership work. But let those be a reflection of the true, lasting joy that comes from a close relationship with the Lord. For leaders, daily joys, perhaps in this gesture or that success, will come and go like reflections. If they are the only source of satisfaction, the work and relationships can easily go sour. Stay close to the Lord so that as the moments go by you can see the true satisfier behind them.

b. Keep yours a partnership in the Gospel.

"I always pray with joy because of your partnership in the gospel from the first day until now" (1:4–5). "It is right for me to feel this way about all of you . . . [because] all of you share in God's grace with me" (1:7).

Pastors and leaders, your partnership will reach its potential only when it is rooted in the Gospel—in the new changed lives you each have through faith in the God who created you, saved you in Christ, and sanctifies you through the Holy Spirit. The partnership will grow in strength as you experience God's grace and as you share in the mission aims of the Gospel and cooperate in making them happen. Without grace experiences and Gospel commitments, a partnership of church leaders will be frail under stress and will be like any other team of people who can share just a small part of themselves.

c. Recognize God as the source of true encouragement, comfort, and spirit.

"If you have any encouragement from being united with Christ, if any comfort from his love, if any fellowship with the Spirit . . . (2:1).

The joy of a partnership of leaders includes things like giving each other encouragement and comfort and having a good spirit, as will be developed later. But leaders must recognize that these experiences can be on a different and much more profound level in church life. Encouragement from being alive in Christ is so much more powerful than giving or getting a pat on the back. The comfort drawn from Christ's love is all-embracing and not something that might be quickly withdrawn. A spirit of togetherness goes much deeper when it comes from fellowship with the Holy Spirit.

Christians have the ingredients for a leadership partnership of joy that, when well used, can far overshadow any other work

165

relationships the participants might have as a point of reference. It can be the best of any togetherness you have experienced.

2. In partnership, keep your sights set high and beyond yourselves.

If your purpose for coming together as leaders is to satisfy your personal interests and to perpetuate what you already have, your joy together will be limited. The partnership will miss what can elevate it to new, previously unknown heights.

a. See your own needs from the perspective of service to others.

"Do nothing out of selfish ambition or vain conceit, but in humility consider others better than yourselves. Each of you should look not only to your own interests, but also to the interests of others" (2:3, 4).

Paul describes this as the attitude to be learned from Christ Jesus himself. Jesus did not insist on His high status as God but humbled himself, took on the nature of a servant, and was obedient to His task, even when that meant the personal loss by death on the cross. God then gave Him high honors, but that was because of what He did as a servant (2:5–11).

Jesus did not emphasize the status and rights of His office, and neither should His leaders. Especially in churches Christians are called to be servant leaders. This is the necessary attitude for a partnership of joy.

b. Let your insights and decisions flow from love.

"This is my prayer: that your love may abound more and more in knowledge and depth of insight, so that you may be able to discern what is best . . . (1:9–10).

The affairs of a church often have to be conducted with a knowledge base, values, and decision processes similar to those used elsewhere. But having that happen out of a context and commitment to love makes the church leader partnership different. When in doubt, go back to what would be the most loving. To become a better church leader, abound in love.

c. Think big and high. Keep the partnership challenged.

"Finally, brothers, whatever is true, whatever is noble, whatever is right, whatever is pure, whatever is lovely, whatever is admirable—if anything is excellent or praiseworthy—think about such things" (4:8).

Joy comes especially from doing what is noble, lovely, ad-

mirable, and excellent, as well as true, right, pure, and praiseworthy. Be sure that individual leaders and groups reach out to
find and recognize what is perhaps more noble, admirable, and
excellent than what a church fellowship is currently doing. That
is how the joy of new worthwhile endeavors begins and expands.

3. Exercise partnership by encouraging each other.

a. Share the confidence that comes from doing the Lord's
work.

"[I am] confident of this, that he who began a good work in
you will carry it on to completion until the day of Christ Jesus"
(1:6).

Paul is certainly referring to the good work of salvation that
God started and carried on in each believer. That is truly a source
of confidence of which to remind each other. But in the same
sentence Paul is speaking of the partnership in the Gospel, which
we see with special meaning for the leaders. Remind each other
to be confident that God will see through to completion His work
done through them.

b. Assure each other of the Lord's strength that can meet
all needs.

"I [and you] can do everything through him who gives me
strength" (4:13).

"My God will meet all your needs according to his glorious
riches in Christ Jesus" (4:19).

Does the job seem too much or the problems too great? Together you can find strength you never dreamed you had. God
has riches enough to meet your needs.

4. Exercise partnership by comforting each other.

Church leadership is not without its trials, as all who have
done it know. When these happen, Paul advises:

a. Stand by each other.

"Stand firm in one spirit, contending as one man for the faith
of the gospel without being frightened in any way by those who
oppose you" (1:27–28).

Standing firm in one spirit is partnership at its best. The act
of standing beside a person who is being tested is basic to the
Greek word for comfort. What this means for partnership is described elsewhere by Paul when he praises "the God of all comfort, who comforts [stands by] us in all our troubles, so that we

167

can comfort [stand by] those in any trouble with the comfort we ourselves have received from God" (2 Cor. 1:3).

b. Pray together, especially in times of stress.

"Do not be anxious about anything, but in everything, by prayer and petition, with thanksgiving, present your requests to God. And the peace of God, which transcends all understanding, will guard your hearts and your minds in Christ Jesus" (Phil. 4:6–7).

Help each other trust God to grant the peace that may be so greatly needed by one or all. Prayer is one of the best ways to give help.

5. Work hard to settle disagreements.

Fellowship with the one Holy Spirit should produce a firm, united spirit among those in partnership. Disagreements that grow from being tolerably minor to divisively major can tear away at that joyful unity. Paul offers several pointers on increasing agreement by decreasing disagreements.

a. Keep talking to each other in the face of conflict.

"I plead with Euodia and I plead with Syntyce to agree with each other in the Lord. Yes, I ask you, loyal yokefellow, help these women who have contended at my side in the cause of the gospel" (4:2–3).

Even among the beloved Philippian leaders there were disagreements. One way or the other it will happen in all partnerships. Left unattended, such conflict can drain the joy. Knowing this, Paul insisted that others take responsibility to seek resolution, to be blessed peacemakers. Such help should be given for the sake of those in conflict but also for the sake of the lasting joy of the leaders' partnership.

b. But remember to appreciate the blessings of diversity.

To the Corinthians Paul wrote: "God has arranged the parts in the body, every one of them, just as he wanted them to be. If they were all one part, where would the body be? As it is, there are many parts, but one body" (1 Cor. 12:18–20).

Differences among church members can ruin a fellowship. But the basic problem is not the differences themselves. It is how they are viewed and handled. For Paul, the challenge in an overall fellowship is to keep looking for the points of unity that will hold the members together *with* their diversity, not just in spite of it.

Paul's source of energy and enthusiasm for dealing with diversity was his understanding of the church as the body of Christ with many parts. What kind of body would it be if all were the same bodily organ—an eye, an ear, or a nose? A considerably deprived one, he notes, without perhaps the ability to hear or a sense of smell or maybe no feet to walk on. Nor should there even be debate about which organs to favor. God has arranged them just as He wanted. Unity cannot be found in the sameness of parts. It is in the one God and Spirit into which the members are baptized and in whom the members partake. With this teaching as his platform, Paul could confront the bad that occurs with the good of God-given diversity among Christians.

c. Confront resistance, speaking the truth in love.

"Instead, speaking the truth in love, we will in all things grow up into him who is the Head, that is, Christ" (Eph. 4:15).

An abundance of diversity, nevertheless, can be a mixed blessing. Especially when church leaders pursue a shared vision, diversity that turns into conflict becomes unwelcome resistance. Recognize it and deal with it was Paul's working principle, as seen in his actions among the Corinthians. To the Ephesians he expressed the basic step as speaking the truth in love. Then all will grow up into Christ together.

Partnerships can best find joy by looking beyond themselves for their purpose. In conflict Christian leaders have to learn to do that by growing up into Him who is the Head, Christ. Such growth happens most consistently by facing the truth, however painful. So speak it. But do so in love.

6. Pastors, show the other leaders that you care for them.

Pastor, do the other leaders in your church know where they stand with you? Do they feel that they are being tolerated by someone who would prefer to be elsewhere or to have other colleagues? They will find more joy and thus you will find more joy in a partnership where each cares for the others and shows it.

a. Look forward to time with your leaders and learn about them.

"God can testify how I long for all of you" (Phil. 1:8).

"My brothers, you whom I love and long for . . . (4:1).

"I hope in the Lord Jesus to send Timothy to you soon, that I also may be cheered when I receive news about you" (2:19).

Unlike imprisoned Paul, you need not depend on someone else to find out what is happening in the lives of your leaders.

Ask them directly. Take the time to get to know them better personally. Show that you care about them.

b. Make it evident that you put their welfare first.

"[Rather than depart to be with Christ], I know that I will remain, and I will continue with all of you for your progress and joy in the faith, so that through my being with you again your joy in Christ Jesus will overflow on account of me" (1:25–26).

Pastor, how have you shown that you want to make a difference in their lives, that their joy is important to you, and that you want to be part of that joy?

c. Do specific actions to lessen their worries and make them glad.

"Therefore I am all the more eager to send him [Epaphroditus], so that when you see him again you may be glad and I may have less anxiety" (2:28).

The Philippian leaders were worried about Epaphroditus and his health after they sent him to help take care of Paul in his imprisonment. Paul sent him back, probably to deliver this letter of remembrance and care but especially to allay their anxiety about him. With the sending of both the letter and Epaphroditus, the Philippians could not help but feel how deeply Paul cared for them.

What and how can you, pastor, send messages to leaders of your church that show how much you care for them?

d. Look for what will make them look good.

"Not that I am looking for a gift, but I am looking for what may be credited to your account" (4:17).

The Philippians treated Paul well. He could not help but like them. Yet most important to him were not the tangible gifts they gave him. It was how well their unusual generosity reflected on them. This was a poor church, but they were moved to give freely of what they had. God and Paul recognized this wonderful fruit. Paul went out of his way to boast of it, especially to the Corinthians (2 Cor. 8:1–5).

Have your church and its leaders done something exceptional for which you can boast? Find those things and talk about them. It is important for other churches to know what can be done. It is just as important for your leaders to know that you are pleased and excited about them.

7. Leaders, care for your pastor and show it.

Leaders, what impressions does your pastor have about the regard you leaders have? Is the pastor affirmed, or do you share mostly complaints and implied criticisms? Is your pastor left to feel mostly alone, or is there a real partnership of leaders? Learn from what the Philippian leaders did.

a. Show your concern in visible and specific ways.

"I rejoice greatly in the Lord that at last you have renewed your concern for me. Indeed, you have been concerned, but you had no opportunity to show it" (Phil. 4:10).

"Epaphroditus, . . . who is also your messenger, whom you sent to take care of my needs" (2:25).

"Yet it was good of you to share in my troubles" (4:14).

Paul was in prison in Rome at the time of this letter and separated by distance. But he was not separated in thought from them or by them. We do not know what else the Philippians did for Paul, but they did send Epaphroditus to help him. Thus they did what they could to take care of his needs. They shared in his troubles. Your pastor may feel in one kind of prison or another, worried about church problems or personal problems, anxious about being a better leader or becoming more confident of the path God has laid out. Do you know of any such needs? Have you shown you care? The burden of pastoral leadership is heavy. Are you eager to help when there is opportunity?

b. Be generous in financially recognizing the contribution of your pastor. "Moreover, as you Philippians know, in the early days of your acquaintance with the gospel, when I set out from Macedonia, not one church shared with me in the matter of giving and receiving, except you alone; for even when I was in Thessalonica, you sent me aid again and again when I was in need" (4:15–16).

"The matter of giving and receiving" was a business phrase of those days and describes the reckoning of what was received and therefore owed. In addition to all the other dimensions of this work, a pastor's contribution to a church has value that can be reckoned in dollars, using a number of criteria. Whatever the specifics, does the salary you pay show a high value placed on what the pastor is doing?

The Philippians were a poor church, and yours may perhaps be so, too. But a true leaders' partnership of joy must show a high value placed on the contribution each makes. Do that for your pastor as well as you can.

c. Make your pastor proud of you.

"My brothers, you whom I love and long for, my joy and crown . . ." (4:1).

"[Act so you may] become blameless and pure, children of God without fault in a crooked and depraved generation, in which you shine like stars in the universe as you hold out the word of life—in order that I may boast on the day of Christ that I did not run or labor for nothing" (2:15–16).

The true source of joy for a Christian is doing the Lord's will. Also, a partnership of leaders finds its fullest joy in doing the Lord's will together for themselves and the church they are leading.

"Leaders, first and foremost be exemplary Christians. Let your goodwill and fairness be evident (4:5). Whatever happens, conduct yourselves worthy of the Gospel of Christ" (1:27).

Then work that your church may be exemplary. Of course, this should not be done just to make the pastor happy. Yet pastors cannot help but judge their worth by what happens to the congregation. Strive to be effective. When the pastor has you for a joy and crown and the assurance that all the labor was not in vain, the partnership grows and the joy grows.

d. Complete the joy by striving to be like-minded.

"Then make my joy complete by being like-minded, having the same love, being one in spirit and purpose" (2:2).

The joy is started when the leaders themselves have encouragement through Christ, comfort from His love, and fellowship with the Spirit (v. 1). No partnership of church leaders can be truly effective and satisfying without each member being renewed in Christ through the working of the Spirit. Tenderness and compassion should be one result (v. 1), as well as commitment and fervor.

Then complete the joy (the pastor's and yours) by strengthening the partnership. Strive to be like-minded, to think about the same things. This is often hard to do among energetic leaders who individually have many ideas. Accentuating tenderness and compassion will help. Joyful like-mindedness can flow from working again and again to have the same love in Christ. You can commit yourself to be one in spirit and overall purpose and not to be satisfied until you see yourselves approaching such unity. Certainly, at a minimum, "do nothing out of selfish ambition or vain conceit" (v. 3).

Strive to be one with the pastor in a partnership of leaders. Do not be satisfied until it becomes a partnership that all can enjoy—the pastor and each leader. Rejoice, and again, rejoice.

8. Salute each other regularly and often.

"Salute every saint in Christ Jesus. . . . All the saints salute you" (4:21 KJV).

Pastor and all leaders, take time for formal opportunities to affirm each other. Make a ceremony of it. Here is one you can try:

(*Before beginning this exchange, designate leaders to read the 8 statements for*

> *Leader A [President?]*
> *Leader B [Chair?]*
> *Leader C [Chair?]*
> *Leader D [Other].*

The statements begin in the section "Calling on God to Inspire Us.")

A Celebration of Mutual Support for Church Leaders

Pastor: I salute you, co-workers, as partners with me in the Gospel of our Lord Jesus Christ.

Leaders: And we salute you with joy as one given to us by God for our work together in Christ's church.

Pastor: Let us celebrate our ministry and affirm one another in a spirit of mutual appreciation for the blessings God gives to us through one another.

Leaders: Amen. Let us do so with joy!

Our Partnership Is Spiritually Based

Pastor: "I rejoice greatly in the Lord over you."

Leaders: We rejoice in you also, Pastor. Our joy is in the Lord, who has given you to us.

Pastor: I pray for you. I pray with joy because of your partnership with me in the Gospel.

Leaders: We pray for you also. You share the grace of God with us.

Pastor: How good it is that we hold each other up to the Lord! He is the source of our encouragement. He brings us comfort. He provides us with His Spirit.

173

Leaders: Thank you for reminding us of Him. Indeed, He is the provider of all that we need in our partnership. We lift up the same Lord to you. He brings you encouragement, comfort, and His Spirit.

Our Mutual Confession and Absolution

Pastor: I need to confess to you, my partners, that I have not always spoken and thought as kindly of you as I should. Sometimes I have complained. Sometimes I have been too focused on my own thoughts and ideas to listen well to yours. Sometimes I have failed to pray for you. Sometimes I have withheld from you the word of encouragement and appreciation that you needed. Sometimes I have looked to my own interest above yours. Forgive me for Jesus' sake.

Leaders: You have been washed. You have been sanctified. The blood of Jesus Christ has covered all your sins and weaknesses. In His name and by His power we forgive you. Live in the joy of the Lord.

We also confess to you. We have not always spoken and thought as kindly of you as we should. Sometimes we have let you down. Sometimes we have criticized you unjustly. Sometimes we have not listened or heeded the words you have shared with us from the Lord. Sometimes we have assumed that you do not need words of affirmation and encouragement in your ministry. Forgive us for Jesus' sake.

Pastor: You have been washed. You have been sanctified. The blood of Jesus Christ has covered all your sins and weaknesses. In His name and by His power I forgive you. Live in the joy of the Lord.

Our Commitment to Each Other of Care and Support

Pastor: I pledge to you, dear leaders, my prayers that God will move in you daily, filling you with His indescribable love, increasing your knowledge of Him, and giving you a spirit of true wisdom. I recognize that you face many competing claims for your attention and energy, and I ask that God give you a generous portion of His wisdom and strength in meeting them.

I pledge faithfulness by God's power in assuring you of the Lord's attempt to meet all our needs in this congregation. The Lord has brought us together, and He will bring to completion what He has begun in us.

Leaders: And we pledge to you our prayers in this partnership. We recognize that your task is not easy. When your life is filled with stress, we will remind you by the Lord's power of the peace of God, which transcends all understanding, for it will guard your heart and mind in Christ Jesus.

We further pledge to work with you to settle disagreements quickly, to keep communicating in the face of conflict, to appreciate the particular gifts God has given you, and to speak the truth in love.

Together: We pledge to each other, by the might of the Spirit, our bond of love and support.

Calling on God to Inspire Us

Pastor: Father, you have blessed us with one another. We, the leaders of your church here gathered, give You thanks and praise for entrusting us with the ministry of the Gospel.

Leaders: We praise you, O God, and magnify Your glorious name.

Leader A: We praise You that despite our weaknesses, You see fit to make us gifts to your church and have endowed us with all the spiritual gifts needed for ministry in this place.

Leaders: We praise You, O God, and magnify Your glorious name.

Leader B: We praise You for the contribution each of us makes to the body of Christ, for our different personalities and skills, for our responsibilities, and for the confidence our congregation has put in us to be leaders in this church.

Leaders: We praise You, O God, and magnify Your glorious name.

Leader C: We flee to you, O Jesus, Son of God and Son of Man, with our feelings of inadequacy.

Leaders: Precious Savior, have mercy on us.

Leader D: We flee to you with our failures, our sporadic zeal, our hesitant commitment.

Leaders: Precious Savior, have mercy on us.

Pastor: We flee to You, dear Lord, with our less than perfect vision for Your church and our reluctance to give our all for the spreading of the Gospel.

Leaders: Precious Savior, have mercy on us.

Pastor: Spirit of the Living God, fill us with a passion for the Gospel and for Your church. Fan into flame the gifts You have given to us.

Leaders: Ignite us with zeal and love.

Leader A: Call us to the highest standards, Holy Spirit, so that we might reach the full stature of Christ.

Leaders: Holy Spirit, hear us.

Leader B: Remove by your graciousness, O Spirit, all discord and strife, all slander and gossip, all quarreling and contention from our midst.

Leaders: Purge us by your power, Spirit of truth and love.

Leader C: Make us daring leaders, willing to risk great things and personal involvement for the Gospel's sake. Do not let us faint for fear of failure nor give up the vision when the way is tough.

Leaders: Encourage us, Spirit of God.

Leader D: And should we ever border on despair, tire of contending for the faith, or be tempted to let the strain defeat us, rise up within us with Your might and renew us.

Leaders: Renew us with divine power, O Holy Spirit.

Pastor: And finally, O Father, Son and Spirit, bind us whom you have called to be leaders in Your church into a mutual bond of love and support, that we might befriend each other at all times, lift one another up in prayer, speak encouragingly to one another, and celebrate with great joy our partnership in the Gospel.

Leaders: O Father, Son and Spirit, God eternal and ever blessed, hear us and grant this petition.

Pastor: O Lord,

Leaders: have mercy on us.

Pastor: O Christ,

Leaders: hear us.

Pastor: O Lord,

Leaders: grant us Your peace.

Together: AMEN.

BV652.1 .L84 1990   CU-Main

Luecke, David S., 1/New designs for church leaders

3 9371 00009 4128